The knowledge contained herein if put into practice can enrich your future, shape your destiny, and turn your aspirations and dreams into a shining and stimulating reality.

IT COULDN'T BE DONE
by Edgar A. Guest

Somebody said that it couldn't be done,
    But he with a chuckle replied
That "maybe it couldn't," but he would be one
    Who wouldn't say so till he tried.
So he buckled right in with the trace of a grin
    On his face. If he worried he hid it.
He started to sing as he tackled the thing
    That couldn't be done, and he did it.

Somebody scoffed: "Oh, you'll never do that,
    At least no one ever has done it;"
But he took off his coat and he took off his hat,
    And the first thing we knew he'd begun it,
With a lift of his chin and a bit of a grin,
    Without any doubting or quiddit,
He started to sing as he tackled the thing
    That couldn't be done, and he did it.

There are thousands to tell you it cannot be done,
    There are thousands to prophesy failure;
There are thousands to point out to you, one by one,
    The dangers that wait to assail you.
But just buckle in with a bit of a grin,
    Just take off your coat and go to it;
Just start to sing as you tackle the thing
    That "cannot be done," and you'll do it.

"Copyright 1934, by the Reilly and Lee Company"

MENTAL POWER

through SLEEP SUGGESTION *and* CONTROLLED RELAXATION

*Two Techniques of Reaching and
Influencing the Subconscious*

by
MELVIN POWERS
*Author
Self-Hypnosis
Dynamic Thinking
Hypnotism Revealed
The Science of Hypnosis
Advanced Techniques of Hypnosis
A Practical Guide to Self-Hypnosis
A Practical Guide to Better Concentration*

Published by
Melvin Powers
WILSHIRE BOOK COMPANY
12015 Sherman Road
No. Hollywood, California 91605
Telephone: (213) 875-1711 / (818) 983-1105

> *Printed by*
> HAL LEIGHTON PRINTING COMPANY
> P.O. Box 3952
> North Hollywood, California 91605
> Telephone: (213) 983-1105

Copyright 1952

by

Melvin Powers

All rights reserved. No part of this book may be reproduced in any form without permission in writing from the publisher, except by a reviewer who wishes to quote brief passages in connection with a review written for inclusion in a magazine, newspaper, radio, or television broadcast.

Printed in the United States of America
Library of Congress Catalog Card Number: 57-12940

ISBN 0-87980-097-6

CONTENTS

Foreword 7

Chapter One
The Problem of Tension 10

Chapter Two
The Way to Happiness and Maturity 21

Chapter Three
Life's Fulfillment Through Controlled Relaxation ... 37

Chapter Four
The Subconscious Mind in Action 55

Chapter Five
The Power of Suggestion 63

Chapter Six
Mental-Therapy Through Sleep Suggestion 73

Chapter Seven
Memory Development While You Sleep 82

Chapter Eight
The Secret of Achieving Success and Happiness 93

Chapter Nine
The Sleep-o-matic Units, the Instruments
    for Releasing Subconscious Power 104

FOREWORD

THIS BOOK has been specifically designed for those who have neither the time nor the inclination for extensive study. Its purpose is to point out and explain the features of our techniques of sleep suggestion and controlled relaxation and to use these new insights to the end that life and living become a richer and happier experience.

The suggestions contained in this book are couched in a language so positive and constructive that a proper reading and understanding of its content cannot but help create new feelings of confidence, courage, and enthusiasm in those who have seldom experienced these sensations before.

It has only been within the last few years that scholars have become aware of the possibilities of sleep therapy and sleep suggestion. Independent researchers in the fields of learning and therapy have reported marvelous progress in these exciting new areas.

These new techniques of sleep learning and controlled relaxation are effective in reaching the subconscious mind, and therefore can be used to awaken its tremendous power for such purposes as achieving success, happiness, and glowing health. We are all aware of the unlimited potential of the subconscious mind. With our new techniques of reaching it, we can achieve undreamed of strength and satisfactions. The power of these techniques is derived from the skillful use of constructive suggestion which aids in opening up new spiritual and mental frontiers for those who aspire to achieve them.

Who of us is not influenced by the tremendous power of suggestion? Negative suggestions can be the cause of invalidism, while positive ones can bring good health and happiness. Suggestions can heal and they can destroy. It is within your power to choose your own destiny!

We know that a man can rise from failure to success if he is fortified with the proper suggestions. He is in a sense in this manner reborn. The quality of his mind remains the same and yet a basic change has come about because he has been taught to think constructively. There are literally thousands of people who have achieved their goals through the effective use of the dynamics of positive thinking, suggestion, auto-suggestion, hypnotism, self-hypnosis, sleep suggestion, and controlled relaxation.

Our techniques of controlled relaxation and sleep suggestion are two remarkably efficient means of attaining great development, not only because of the singular efficiency of the methods used, but because we have incorporated in our methods the accepted findings of all the scholars in the field of psychology. The key to this achievement lies in the manner by which we are able through suggestion to contact the subconscious mind, which as we know is active both during the waking moments of the day, as well as during the hours of sleep at night. This book then is dedicated to the purpose of discussing the nature of those contacts and an analysis of the techniques which makes those contacts possible.

For the sake of avoiding any confusion we are treating these two techniques separately. The first technique, that of controlled relaxation will not be discussed after the end of the third chapter so that in effect this book will be composed of two parts. The first three chapters are devoted to the discussion of the technique of controlled relaxation, while in the last six chapters we will be solely pre-occupied with the technique of sleep suggestion. We have elected to devote more space to the latter only because of the greater novelty and complexity of its approach, and not because we in any way deem it superior to the former. The reader is not to assume that we in any way favor the latter technique. Each is equally important. Each is equally vital! It will be the task of the reader to select the one that he deems most acceptable to himself.

MELVIN POWERS

12015 Sherman Road
No. Hollywood, California 91605

CHAPTER I

The Problem of Tension

"Half the spiritual difficulties that men and women suffer arise from the morbid state of health." H. W. Beecher.

WE LIVE in a frightening and wonderful age! Our world is in a state of perpetual crisis! All our resources, both personal and impersonal, are being taxed to the utmost, and yet no one knows where we are going, and where it will all end! Our lives are tense with the pressures of today, and the added fears of an unknown tomorrow. We are living in a period of emotional contagion in which fears, both real and imagined, are robbing us of our cherished peace of mind. We live in an age of crisis in which the condition of relaxation has become the exception rather than the rule. A period, in fact, in which tensions prevail as the major condition of our confused lives, while peace and ease of heart and mind have vanished like the silver notes of a Victorian love song.

Any serious student of the social sciences knows that the size and the make up of a country's population

THE PROBLEM OF TENSION

is vitally important in the consideration of a nation's political, economic, and military power. He knows also that the quality of a people is a vital and primary consideration in a nation's welfare. Wars have today become largely psychological; therefore such qualities as morale, leadership, and group and individual solidarity take on a greater importance today than ever before in the preservation of a nation's existence. A nation's ability to withstand the enemy's psychological pressure is vitally necessary to its continued welfare and security in the future.

In the light of these facts doesn't a people's health and its physical welfare take on more importance than it ever had before? The people of a nation are its greatest asset. Without them nothing can function; with them a nation can flourish and grow great. The populace then is the greatest treasure of a nation. Since the people are composed of individuals, it is the welfare of the individual in the last analysis that is of the utmost importance to a nation. It is that individual and his welfare that we are going to discuss in the ensuing pages.

Our society is indeed a very complex one! It has become so highly organized that the strain of just getting along has become all but insurmountable. People have become so nervous mentally and physically that our society is in danger of a collective breakdown. The mad race for success, and the sheer struggle for existence have proved so enervating that our people are rapidly becoming "nervous wrecks." Millions of people are unable to sleep because of nervousness, and so find it difficult to get through the working day. Imagine what this is doing to our industrial efficiency and social relationships!

It is time that we paid closer attention to the welfare of our bodies and the condition of our minds! Our minds and bodies are our basic sources of strength! To disregard their welfare and condition is to court the danger of severe illness and the eventual disruption of our society! Our teachers, our professional men, our leaders of business and industry must be made more aware of the relationship between personal ease, body vitality, and the welfare of our society!

It is undoubtedly true that environmental and economic factors are frequently the cause of despair and tension in the individual, but it is also true that these conditions can arise out of his own small regard for his own health. The intelligent individual makes his adjustments with a careful calculation for his personal welfare. He watches his sleep and relaxation periods, does not worry needlessly, does not expend energy uselessly, and takes all precautions necessary to insure his good health. Of what use is man to himself or society if his health is poor? Besides, excessive tension, and the lack of sufficient rest can result in both the physical and psychological disintegration of the individual. What could be worse than that?

Tension is visible in many ways, both physical and psychological. Some complain of physical disturbances

THE PROBLEM OF TENSION

such as aches and pains, while others walk about in a constant state of annoyance and anxiety making themselves and those about them unhappy with their wailing and protestations. Others, who are equally as tense, do not appear nervous at all, but restrain themselves sufficiently to hide their nervousness. These people are probably worse off than the complainers because the the former through their complaints are at least getting some of that harmful pressure out of their systems.

The physical conditions that arise out of tension are many. Restrictions of joint flexibility, poor circulation, and disturbances in the digestive system are only a few of the organic disorders. In the psychological realm, conditions like lack of concentration, poor memory, insomnia, overactivity, and irritability are the resultant manifestations of tension. In order to remain at ease and relaxed, it is necessary to find the proper balance between work, recreation, and rest. This balance must, in fact, be maintained if health, vitality, and peace of mind are to be insured. The establishment, therefore, of a rhythm of living based on this behavioral triangle is necessary to the continued stability and welfare of the individual.

In a psychological sense, anxieties and tension show themselves in conflict. The unfortunate individual is torn between two opposing drives each of which wants expression. A normal person is able to make a choice rather easily, while the anxiety ridden one flounders, and is in fact, involved in a situation in which he has no free wheeling whatsoever. This leaves him in a state of continued debilitation and despair which persists until he gains temporary relief by an evasion of the problem, or better still by completely solving his dilemma.

The problem of conflict and tension is not a new one in our society. The dramas, philosophies, and religions of ancient civilizations paid much attention to, and evinced much concern over the problem of conflict and its effect, tension. Their ways of expressing the problem was, of course, much different than our more modern scientific approach to the matter. They clothed the dilemma in such symbolic ideas as God and the devil, the forces of light and darkness, and good and evil. We today, due to the modern psychological approach of Dr. Sigmund Freud and other major psychologists, have a much clearer and more personal, and scientific understanding of conflict and its tensions.

It was Freud's theory, and of course this knowledge is a commonplace today, that our basic conflicts are those between our instinctual drives and their demands for expression, on the one hand, and the restrictions which our society sets up against their fulfillment on the other. The frustration, fear, guilt, and aggression that arise from this dilemma cause us to become anxiety ridden, and ultimately so tense and fatigued that we can be rightfully classified as neurotics if this condition tends to persist. It is not true, however, to say that all who are tense or unrelaxed are neurotic. That would be an untenable position to defend indeed because certain situations create tensions that vanish as soon as the problem is solved.

THE PROBLEM OF TENSION

It is important to remember that man is a total organism. The body as well as the mind are dual aspects of the total personality. Haven't we all had the experience of having an annoying headache ruin our pleasures or found ourselves feeling "blue" because we had a backache or some other type of ailment that ruined our dispositions for the time being? Are these examples not indications of the inter-relationship between the body and mind? In thinking of tension and anxiety then, it must be remembered that we are involved in both areas.

We have been speaking of tension. I think we had better at this time explain our use of the word, and its meaning, which we have only vaguely mentioned before. As Freud has suggested tension is a condition that results from the body being barraged by emotional stimuli which demand action, but which action seldom or never occurs, because society will not permit the gratification of these impulses. This creates a state of inhibition which leaves both the body and mind in a tense and strained condition. The problem is further complicated and expanded by the fact that there is a persistence in perpetuating attitudes and impulses that tend to keep the body and mind in this tense or strained condition continuously.

This, of course, is not the whole story. As we have already stated, the uncertainty and insecurity of our world, and our part in it, create such fears in us that our existences become ridden with fears and anxieties. The causes are of course multitudinous. Jobs may be uncertain; old age may mean destitution; one's health may be bad; war may seem imminent; the prospect of death may be frightening; self-confidence may be lacking; one fears one's wife may run away with another man, or one's husband may run away with another woman, the future may be frightening; and so on ad infinitum.

It is the nature of fear that it creates tensions that are not relieved unless these problems are solved. If they are not solved anxiety, irritability, and excessive sensitivity inevitably result and a breakdown becomes imminent.

It is interesting to note that symptoms of tension can even result from the practice of inhibiting distressing memories which have proven to be damaging to the pride or vanity of an individual. Since forgetting is only seldom a complete eradication of an idea, and its accompanying emotional patterns, these are merely pushed back into our unconscious mind where they continue to fester and create tension of which we are not consciously aware. These tensions remain in a dormant state until some stimulus causes them to erupt in a seemingly inexplicable manner.

Even sleep does not bring release from tension for many of the anxieties continue to afflict us as the problems of the waking hours spill over into the period of slumber. Sleep becomes restless. Dreams and nightmares destroy the ease and tranquility of the resting hours. The sleeper gets out of a troubled bed unrested,

THE PROBLEM OF TENSION

tense, with muscles and head aching from the strain of tortured dreams. There seems, indeed, no rest for the weary.

The effects of tension are evident in a myriad of ways. I have already suggested a few, but to give a fuller account of the more common symptoms of excessive tension and anxiety, it is necessary to mention distressing heart conditions like shortness of breath, pain, excessive palpitation, and the skipping of heart beats, or high blood pressure, which is dangerous whether organic or functional. Another common symptom is the dysfunction of the gastrointestinal system which includes the stomach, esophagus, tongue, salivary glands, intestines, gall bladder, and the liver. Anyone of these can be disturbed through the presence of persistent tension in the organism. The ears, eyes, and nose are also organs disturbed by these pressures.

Extreme tension also causes speech difficulties. There are at least a million of our population in the United States that are disturbed by speech impediments. Many cures for these impediments have been used ranging from hypnotism, which has done a great deal of good, to voice training, and witchcraft, which was used in our less sophisticated past. The most effective treatment for the alleviation of stuttering, which is one of the more common impediments, is to relieve the sufferer from the basic cause of his tension.

This condition can under certain circumstances make the speech muscles so rigid that they cannot relax sufficiently to make the required sounds for normal speech. The factor of habit is also very important in the continuation of speech deficiencies. The speech pattern once strengthened tends to persist out of sheer momentum. It is interesting to note, however, that once the stutter becomes interested in a subject, he tends to lose his speech inhibitions because since he has become relaxed he proceeds to speak like any other normal person. Of course the personality structure, as well as the environmental factors, must be included in any consideration of the total cure of the unfortunate individual.

The respiratory system is also effected by the presence of excessive tension in the organism. Conditions like asthma, shallow breathing, persistent coughing, hiccoughs, and sighing are frequently observed among the anxiety ridden sufferers. The genito-urinary system can also be effected. Symptoms of tension may become evident through such skin conditions as eczema, psoriasis, and other skin eruptions which are unpleasant both to the afflicted and to the observer. Headaches and insomnia have already been mentioned as conditions rising out of excessive tension states. It is also important to note that any genuine organic ailment will tend to become aggravated because of the presence of tension in the person. Before terminating this dis-

THE PROBLEM OF TENSION

cussion we cannot let this occasion pass without mentioning the conditions that peculiarly effect women who are continuously nervous in their every day activities.

Pregnancy and menstruation are deeply effected by the presence of excessive emotion and disturbance. Menstration starts about the eleventh year and continues until about the age of forty-five. While it is perfectly true that there are physical conditions that tend to aggravate the periods of menstruation and pregnancy, emotional factors causing tension also tend to exacerbate these processes to a very marked degree. This can also result in sexual frigidity, which unfortunately, afflicts many women.

The influence of anxiety is nowhere so obvious as in these functions of menstruation and pregnancy. How the former can be delayed and dislocated has already been suggested, as for the latter, women who are afraid of pregnancy, or those who devoutly desire children, and yet fear they cannot have them, find their menses disturbed and delayed because of these anxieties. It seems to matter little whether the disturbing tension is aroused by fear, or the desire for children, the effects are the same. The normal menstrual periods are disturbed or delayed thus causing more fear and frustration, a vicious cycle indeed. The influence and effects of tension on the matters most vital to women themselves—their periods of menstruation and pregnancy becomes very obvious. These affect not only the women themselves, but their families and ultimately our society, which has no small stake in the health and vitality of its citizenry, both new born and those in various stages of growth.

The matter of tension and anxiety has been gone into superficially, but rather lengthily, to establish the causes and effects of this destructive evil that is creating such damage both to ourselves and society. The pain, suffering, unhappiness, and abominable waste of energy makes this condition the number one enemy of our people. No society can survive unless it has a vital and mature population, which can develop both its own resources, and that of the country in a manner that will redound both to the glory of the people and the nation. None but a dynamic, energetic people can achieve such a goal! Let us now proceed to investigate some of the means by which we can achieve this sense of strength and well-being, both as individuals and, as citizens of a great nation.

CHAPTER II

The Way to Happiness and Maturity

"Happiness consists in the attainment of our desires and in our having only right desires." Augustine.

WE HAVE already stated that happiness depends partly upon the environment in which we live and partly upon ourselves. To be happy, most people require food, clothing, shelter, love, good health, the respect of one's self and of others, and a job that is interesting and constructive. Happiness is usually to be found through these attainments. If any of these are missing, happiness will be difficult to attain indeed. It is, however possible to have achieved all of these and yet remain bereft of happiness. In such a situation the aid of a psychologist or doctor becomes advisable.

To be happy implies the absence of tensions and anxieties that arise out of such emotions as self-pity, self-love, fear, and envy. These are egocentric and in-going impulses that create a self-centeredness that is damaging to the personality and its harmonious development.

One of the greatest defficiencies of egocentricity is

that it destroys interest both in the institution of society and the people in it. Self-love limits the scope and horizons of the individual to his own advantages and interests thereby creating such a limitation of operation that he soon loses contact with other person's needs and aspirations to a very marked degree. Life so limited becomes boring thus losing its zest, meaning, and purpose.

Those whose interests are objective and wide are the lucky and happy ones of this world. Their affections and pre-occupation range as wide as mankind itself, and as a result their lives are varied, warm, and rich with the wonder and beauty of living. These persons have deep affections and are given affection in return, for it is only those that love who are loved. Their lives are an harmonious and inter-related relationship. The man who loves himself and no others has but one admirer, and though that admirer be faithful, he is nevertheless shallow and empty for the love of self is a lonely and futile love indeed! Man is born of love, and it is only through love, that is to say of other people's love, that happiness can be achieved.

The happy, and therefore the relaxed man, lives objectively, and with, and through other people. The unhappy man, who is usually wrapped up in himself, continues to concentrate on the supposed causes of his unhappiness, and finds himself caught in a vortex in which there is no freedom or pleasure. This person, unlike the man with outside interests, really thinks him-

THE WAY TO HAPPINESS AND MATURITY

self inferior and has the conviction that life is not worth living at all. Unhappiness is caused, of course, by the disintegration of the personality in relationship to himself, and to the society in which he lives. On the other hand—the man who feels himself a citizen of the world, and a part of its drama and interest, and thinks of himself as a link in the chain of humanity, finds in this relationship with man a harmony and joy that only the wise and mature can know.

The psychological causes of unhappiness are of course varied. These have, however, a basic similarity inasmuch as they almost always stem from a deprivation of some satisfaction in the past. This satisfaction having once been denied takes on a greater importance than any of the other desires or needs, and results in an unbalance of emphasis and interests in that particular direction at the expense of all other of goals. Life then, becomes a total pre-occupation with that desire and subsequently is narrowed and distorted. If that purpose is not achieved the unhappy one begins to look for other distractions to offset the pangs of failure at having failed to achieve this highly regarded but actually over-stressed purpose. He then may plunge into the greater futility and the escape of drunkedness, or other irrational pleasures, which only cause greater self-hate and frustration.

This vicious circle ofttimes continues until fear and intelligence come to the aid of the stricken man and help him to find the correct path to better concepts and ultimately to a better way of living.

In speaking of unhappiness, and the fears and anxieties that cause it, it is necessary to point out at this time that fear can actually be a friend. Real fear warns us of danger, and is an instrumentality by which we can avoid getting hurt in the future, as we had avoided it in the past. It is through intelligent fear or constraint that we become moral, honest, and stable in order to continue functioning as an acccepted member of society. Fear that was useful to us as children, and which we used as an invaluable tool for our security, had an important and constructive place in the process of our growth. In fact without useful fear or caution we never could have grown at all. These were real and constructive fears. Such constraints were necessary for our health, growth, and welfare. Restraints like not touching a hot stove, or playing on the sidewalk rather than on the street where we might have been hit by automobiles doubtless saved our lives on more than one occasion. To cling to these fears, however, after the use for them has long passed us by is a sure sign of immaturity. How is it possible for adults to be healthy and normal if they permit the fears of childhood to control them in the more mature activities? Stoves are still hot and can therefore still burn, but does that mean that as adults we had better not go near them? Patently not and yet that is how many adults behave, for instance in sexual matters where the childhood taboos still operate and therefore make it difficult, or in some cases impossible for the mature adaptation of the sexes to one another. It

THE WAY TO HAPPINESS AND MATURITY

is essential to happiness that the real fears be discriminated from the imaginary ones in order that life may be lived to the fullest possible degree! It seems so obvious when so simply stated, but it isn't quite so clear in the every day activities of millions of people.

We shall discuss an example of this on a later page. Those who attempt to escape from fear will never conquer it! They will feel persecuted and harried as long as they live. To face it forthrightly, however, even with uncertainty and confusion is to neutralize its terror. To observe the true proportions of this imagined menace is to realize in most instances that its malignant power is a figment of a tortured imagination! Would you defeat fear? Then face that which frightens you whenever it appears! The fact that you confronted the problem head on, and did not as a result experience the expected torture from that exposure, will make you realize as nothing else can that the fear that was expected did not actually exist at all in reality.

Fear has a way of spreading. It cannot be isolated. If a person feels it in one situation, he will find it confronting him in his other activities if he permits it to get strong enough. Fear must be checked by reason at the exact moment that it is experienced in order that the individual may go about his business in a normal manner. To do this, it is necessary to discriminate between fact and fiction, imagination and reality, balanced and destructive behavior. It is only through this method that the differences between imagination and reality can be discerned and acted upon. Here are a few examples of this unnecessary kind of fear. A man's best friend dies. His death was caused by heart disease. He gets panicky! Heart disease! "We were always together," he reflects. "We did the same things, played the same games, always exercised together. My gracious if that much exertion affected his heart it will affect mine too because we certainly had the same kind and amount of exercise! I'd better quit exercising so much, or better still stop completely to insure no future difficulty at all." Rather frenzied and foolish thinking isn't it? To put it more correctly it is not thinking at all, but a kind of hysteria that would have taken much of the richness out of life for that person because he greatly enjoyed the pleasure and relaxation of being out in the air and sun with other sports loving people. In fact, due to the press of his work this was the only exercise and relaxation he could get at all.

His withdrawal from sports, therefore, would have left an unfillable void that would have brought boredom and ill health into his life as a result of the lack of physical exercise and the deep anxiety caused by the fact of his friend's death, and fear that he too would be cut down in the same manner due to his overly active participation in sports. But he is one of the more intelligent ones. He immediately cut off the pangs of anxiety by realizing that his friend had an inheritance different from his own for after all he was a friend and not a brother. He decides to investigate the family background of his dead friend. Finds out by talking to his friend's sister that both their parents had been afflicted

THE WAY TO HAPPINESS AND MATURITY

with heart trouble which had caused their premature deaths. This bit of information and a check into his own geneology leaves him with the assurance that he need not be concerned any further as there are no known traces of coronary difficulty in his family history. He breathes a sigh of relief, becomes more than ever convinced of the importance of reason in human affairs, and continues to enjoy the pleasures of the outdoors as a healthy and sane human being should.

Here is another example of the conquest of fear by reason with the added impetus of love which makes it somewhat different from the previous example. It is a short account of a very attractive and well-educated girl, who had refused several desirable suitors under one pretext or another, but whose true reason for not wanting to marry, a fact which she never admitted, was that she had been reared in a very unhappy home. Her father a successful, but domineering martinet, had made both her mother's and her own life miserable by his constant abuse. She was an only child. Her father had on numerous occasions actually beaten his wife in the presence of his terrified daughter, who when this occurred, fled in hysterical terror to the sanctuary of her bedroom to avoid the assault that she felt would inevitably descend upon her defenseless head. This incident had repeated itself so often that the frightened child developed a deep rooted fear of men and marriage! If her father was brutal all men must be the same her mind told her. As she grew older, she kept men at a cautious distance, but being a highly prepossessing woman she was constantly the object of male attentions. This made it impossible to put them off endlessly. When she considered the man particularly pleasant or attractive she accepted his company, but only for a short time, for she was afraid of becoming too deeply involved in an intimate relationship with any man since the image of her cruel father seldom left her on the occasions of her meetings with the male sex. This pattern continued for a long time until she met a man she really cared for and who deeply loved her in return. All was well between them until he asked for her hand in marriage. This created an ungovernable terror in her, and in spite of her love for him she asked him not to see her anymore. When he protested that he couldn't do that as he loved her deeply, and when he insisted uopn being told what he had done to deserve such banishment, she finally broke down and narrated the frightening and ugly story of her father's life with her mother. He listened with sympathy and understanding, and became increasingly indignant as she unfolded the miserable narrative that she had kept locked within her heart for so long a time.

As time went on because of love and understanding, the tortured girl was made to realize through reason and observation that the father was only one man, and not a desirable one at that, and that he was not at all the prototype of all men. The man she loved, and the married couples she met through him, made her realize how fine and wholesome people were, and how happy marriage could be if approached in an unselfish and mature manner. This girl was fortunate, of course. She found love, but who can deny that she also found reason and liberation through the intelligent application of her mental faculties in an atmosphere of the most patient and understanding devotion of her beloved husband, for they did marry after she passed the nonage of her emotions, and began to see people and the world about her in a more realistic and mature manner. She like the man in the first example found release from fear through the rewarding use of her God given intelligence. We need a more general use of its beneficient power.

We, as human beings, are all creatures of habits. They control us automatically without our recognition of their mechanistic power. These habits, or our attitudes toward them, have an incalulable effect on our state of health and happiness. They come to us largely from our childhood environment. Habits, of course, are essential to life and living both in the physiological and psychological realms. Without them, nothing could be accomplished in the world, personal or impersonal. Imagine the dilemma we would be in if we had to re-learn how to handle a car every time we got in to drive, or imagine a stenographer having to get re-acquainted with the typewriter keys everytime she sat down to type a letter. Nothing would ever get done, would it? Yes our habits are as some sage reminded us, "Ten times stronger than nature." They can be either our friends or enemies. A good habit is a boon; a bad one a demoralizing influence.

MENTAL POWER Through CONTROLLED RELAXATION

To show how powerful a part habits have in our lives, and how automatically they function, let us observe the routine of an average work day for our Mr. Average Man. He automatically gets up when the alarm rings, mechanically gets out of bed, washes and dresses without thinking, eats, reads the paper, and runs to catch the same car at the same time every day. He does that today, did the same thing yesterday, last week and last year, and will do likewise in the years to come. The patterns have become set, automatic and efficient and therefore relieves the individual of the necessity of expending extra thought and energy on these day by day routines.

Our attitudes or dispositions are created in the same manner as habits, and similarly become hardened and automatic with repetition. It is, therefore, important that we develop desirable attitudes for the richest and most constructive kind of thinking, feeling, and living. In a social sense we are actually a totality of these behavior patterns. Since most of these are outgrowth of our early environment, as I have already pointed out, it is essential that children be equipped with reaction patterns and motivations that will give them the best possible opportunity for future social integration in whatever milieu they may find themselves. There are, of course, other factors that enter into the formulation of the personality. The consideration whether a child was the only one in the family or one of several children is an important factor in character formation. The attitude patterns created out of these situations

THE WAY TO HAPPINESS AND MATURITY

can well, and do affect the future role of youngsters in society and their relationship to other people in it. Whether or not a child was proud of his parents, or his neighborhood, or of the school which he attended, or whether or not he had a physical defect, was too tall, or too small, or had a defective brother or sister, or was ashamed of his home, or for a myriad of other reasons, he became unhappy or happy will have an almost indelible effect on the future growth and stability of the youngster. It is vital, therefore, to develop a pattern of desirable characteristics for the future welfare of all our youngsters and to create such conditions that will make the most wholesome growth possible.

It matters little whether our attitudes are the reflection of the viewpoint of others, or whether they grew out of a particular experience, they tend to become automatic and accepted as though they were an organic part of our total personalities. Here, of course, is where the danger lies, for it must be clearly understood that these attitudes have been learned and therefore can be unlearned and changed to more acceptable ones if the original attitudes are considered undesirable. This transformation will, of course, involve a show of will and a new expenditure of energy because it is not a simple task to cope with a habit or attitude that has become strengthened through persistent operation.

Let us proceed to sketchily enumerate some attitudes so that we will have a mutual understanding of what we are talking about when we use the term. These will first be suggested under the heading of mature attitudes, that is those that are desirable, and second immature ones, that is those that are considered harmful and destructive. In this connection let it be said that even a virtue can become a vice if it is carried to an extreme. If it does it no longer fits under the heading of a mature or virtuous attitude since it is only so if it is used with moderation and good sense. Let us take, for example, the altogether mature attitude of forgiveness. Now we all know that this is a mature virtue, and yet what remains of this virtue if it is carried to the extreme of forgiving men like Hitler or Dillinger, the one time gangster, for the killings that they committed? These men cannot be forgiven! Murder is inhuman and can never obviously be condoned!

Attitudes must be rooted in common-sense and reason to have any personal or social value at all or they will defeat the very purpose they have set out to cure namely as in this case the hate and murder, which these men personified so alarmingly. Here then are some of the mature virtues that are so because they speak of reason, and are well-grounded in an understanding of the moral and social realities of both the past and the present. These virtues no doubt will be also valid for the future since these values have been accepted as truths on the basis of their workability and validity in the long history of civilization. Self-respect and respect for others is an example of maturity as are industry, poise, generosity, a sense of humor, self-reliance, tolerance, understanding, and fair-mindedness just to name a few. Are these attitudes not the desirable

THE WAY TO HAPPINESS AND MATURITY

ones that we all admire and dream about achieving because they speak of strength, self-respect, and social acceptance? The manifestations of immaturity and self-destruction like selfishness, overweening pride, extreme humility, resentment, suspiciousness, self-pity, intolerance, hypersensitivity, and inferiority are deplored and yet clung to by most persons as though they were pearls of great worth. Why does this paradox prevail? Surely everyone wants to be mature and well-liked! What is the difficulty? The fact is that most persons refuse to face themselves honestly! We are aware that many people are emotionally disturbed. These people require medical or psychiatric attention and are not our concern here. Our prime interest is the great mass of people who are able to "face themselves," and help themselves through proper self-evaluation, and an honest understanding of their attitudes both as far as they themselves and mankind in general are concerned. Those who make friends rather than enemies of their attitudes, and have only those that work for them rather than against them, will not only be happier, but healthier people, and will find not only self but social acceptance in the wider sphere of their activities.

A mature and therefore happy person is a reasonable person. First of all he likes himself. His ideal of himself is based on a sensible recognition of his capacities. His goals are those that are within reasonable limits of his attainment. He doesn't object at all to recognizing his short-comings, and to offset these he takes advantage of every opportunity to develop his faculties to their fullest possible degree. He disclaims any desire for perfectionism knowing it to be unattainable, but he doesn't, therefore, look upon himself as second rate, but rather strives to function to his utmost limits in a practical and moral manner so that his life can be full and rich in meaning and purpose. He is the wise and happy one for he has learned the meaning of the Confucian principle of moderation in all things! He inevitably must be a healthy, happy productive human being and a credit to himself, his family, and his country for he is himself through reason preparing the way for his mental and spiritual growth.

The wise, happy, and mature man knows that all problems must be faced realistically. When he meets a problem or situation that requires change, he observes all the available facts, and possible solutions, and then after considered reflection and mature (the word is used advisedly) deliberation he adopts whatever methods are required to bring about that desired change. The mature man is aware that there are situations he cannot change. He faces such a dilemma honestly and unemotionally and continues to function within the framework of his limitations without stress or strain until such a time that he can bring about the necessary alteration. He knows that impulses generating from within himself are not so permanent that they cannot be changed through the proper application of his will and intelligence. He does this by going to the very source of the problem, himself, finding here the strength and

THE WAY TO HAPPINESS AND MATURITY

resources to bring about the reformation and integration of his unique personality. It is only through this method that an individual can develop.

The mature man is not a fatalist because he is aware that such an attitude can be an evasion of his responsibilities. He does not solve or evade problems by claiming to be powerless in the face of irresistable reality. His decisions are his own, and he comes to them through careful analysis of the specific situation as it actually exists in fact, and so he ever remains the realist in his preoccupations with the world around him. The mature man does not live in the past, but rather prepares for the future by attending to his day to day problems constructively with the fullest sense of the continuity of time. He is not afraid of failure! He knows that defeat may be necessary to growth and future happiness because it can expose the causes of his errors and demonstrate how to avoid them in the future. His dreams are real because he keeps them within the sphere of his attainment! He scorns mere satisfaction of the moment. He is too concerned with the long view of achievement and happiness to pick up the dead flowers that lie in the path to his goal when the beauty and redolence of live roses beckon him in the future. He is not a stiff-necked moralist, for he enjoys fun and laughter in his day to day experiences, and looks questioningly upon those that find no joy in living.

The mature man does not judge people by their bank accounts or possessions. He interests himself in the real person before him rather than in the superficial and extraneous considerations that go to make up the usual judgments of people. He is friendly, outgoing, democratic, and hospitable in the true sense of the word. It is his pleasure to make anybody and everybody feel at home with him. He is interested in personal growth, and is at all times able to adjust himself to changing circumstances. He is an optimist, not foolishly but realistically, because he knows that dynamic energy is at the very source of life, and that its force is for good if used constructively. He has learned to take life calmly, and only permits his emotions to function when the occasion calls for it, and the situation justifies it. He sees life philosophically and appreciates the beauty and wonder of it because he knows it is great to be alive and a human being! He is in short, the happy man, the mature man, the finest creation of nature and God!

CHAPTER III

Life's Fulfillment Through Controlled Relaxation

"To help the young soul, to add energy, inspire hope and blow the coals into a useful flame; to redeem defeat by new thought and firm action, this, though not easy, is the work of divine men." **Emerson.**

MAN IS EVER in search of a way to surmount the frustrations and limitations of his personality and the world around him. The experiences of his every day living leave him with a sense of helplessness and the accompanying wish that he could somehow burst the bonds of his inhibitions so that he could better cope with himself and the oppressive environment in which he revolves. In short he wants to find some means by which he can enlarge his own potential so that he, and the world in which he lives, can become much better.

This striving for greater development and expansion is at the core of all human motivation, and becomes increasingly evident as we observe history and the sciences. Knowledge, they say, is power, money is power, prestige is power, fame is power, and so we could run through the gamut of human achievement to show an irresistable drive for power and self-expression. This drive for growth and expression is at the very source of our beings, and is the motivation behind the rise of our civilization. Individuals, as well as societies, grow through the impulse of the organism for development. The stages of our biological growth from the passivity of the embryo to the activity of the mature person are clear evidence, both in nature and in ourselves, that life means growth and expanding self-independence, or it means nothing at all but pointless disintegration and death.

To live, man must grow and express himself, or he will pay the price in physical illness or psychological decadence. There is a wonderful, dynamic power in man! It is his task to utilize that power for the sake of the fullest development of his uniqueness. Man must express this urge for articulation, or he becomes like a clod, less than human. What happens to those people who are so frustrated in face of their limitations that they can stand neither themselves nor the world around them? They find other means of expression or rather illusions of expressions. They resort to alcohol or dope which gives them temporary surcease from the ugliness of their lives, and the impotence of their natures. Under the influence of these narcotics they take on tremendous and God-like proportions of illimitable power that they never have known before or can know in the normal humdrum of everyday living. This to us is unquestionable evidence of an overwhelming desire to break the bonds of ordinary limitations even though the means are those which no sane person would ever recommend. The purpose remains clear. It is the desire for release, and the illusion of achievement that these poor, benighted souls cannot achieve in the ordinary ways.

There are other and better ways to find expression. They are in the creative arts of music, literature, the dance, and other art forms in which creation and expression are merged into a form and pattern that are among the highest achievements and noblest expressions of mankind. These along with social pursuits like business and the professions are constructive pursuits necessary to our society. This is the way in which the dreams and fantasies of man can be molded into such patterns as to express the divinity of man, and the creativity and power of the dynamic life force that is God, or the cosmic consciousness, or whatever you personally prefer to call it. This force exists! It is the task of all of us to tune in on it, and so find this power that we have never known before! This is not a mystic force necessarily! It is one of self-conscious intellect, emotion, and intuition that is a part of the larger consciousness of the cosmos. Man is after all a finite part of the infinite mind of the universe!

Human life is, as we already have shown, a process of growth. The experiences that we have are tied together by the chain of memory which links the past to the present and the future. Through this memory a rational order of behavior or sequence is set up to give meaning and purpose to our lives. It is the mind, and one of its factors the memory, that makes us human and therefore superior to the animals whose yesterdays, todays, and tomorrows are only a continued play of imbedded reflexes or instincts that have remained static and permanent for millions of years. Their instincts serve them in place of what they do not have and actually do not need, for their individual and collective existence is based on only the desire for self-preservation. I am not attempting here to demonstrate that man is devoid of instincts, he has a few basic ones. I am merely attempting to demonstrate that man is unique and capable of a time sense and creativity because he has a mind and memory which makes it possible for him to learn and to remember what he has learned in the past. This of course is not the place to enter into the argument whether we as human beings have more or fewer instincts. We will merely state, at this point, that human behavior is not only a totality of either his physical being or experience or learning. We suggest that human behavior is a composite of various degrees of both inheritance and experience, and that is as far as we care to go in the matter, except to say that without the presence of some instincts man would have been badly handicaped in the struggle for existence if in losing instincts he had not gained intelligence to offset that loss, and further to point out that intelligence, in contradistinction to instinct, is not a faculty to do any one thing but the ability to use reason and analysis in coping with specific and general problems as they arise. If human behavior, like animal instinct were completely mechanical, intelligence would never have had an opportunity to function at all. There never would have been developed in man the ability to discriminate between cause and effect. It is this ability that has made him the finest flowering of nature—the king of all he surveys, and therefore superior to animals who live by their instincts alone.

Man because of his intelligence can grow. He does so as he solves problems and brings the wide scope of the world's dilemmas to his mental door, as it were, and finds solutions for them. Through these achievements he gets a fuller understanding of his own capabilities, and therefore learns to direct his energies consciously to the end of the greater self-development of his personality. This is the richest and fullest achievement of human personality, but is so only if the ends sought are productive and beneficial both to himself and mankind. Those, of course, who prefer the security and ease of safety cannot hope to find an expansion of their personality under these passive conditions since growth comes only through the courage of meeting and conquering those problems that press upon us and await our solution. A withdrawal from them may bring temporary peace and relaxation, but since it is not in the nature of problems to solve themselves, the temporary withdrawal from them has in reality solved nothing.

The mind, this wonderful instrument which sets us apart from the animals and makes us superior to them, is the means through which we develop our personalities and so find true freedom. This mind, of course, cannot be considered apart from the total organism of the human being. Its prime purpose and service to the individual lies in its power to direct and expand the mental and spiritual horizons of its possessor and to make it possible for him to find security and growth.

The mind then is capable of intelligence which is, as we see it, the constructive orientation of our energies. It is this intelligence and the correct use of our energies that we are stressing here in the discussion of our two techniques of mental and spiritual development. Our energies must be so directed that they will bring us the benefits that the intelligence wants us to attain because these goals are desirable for us. The intelligence using the energy of the life force in the organism overcomes whatever obstacles lies in the path of its objective, and so becomes even stronger and more expansive. This life force when it is unresisted loses its power for it takes resistance to sharpen and strengthen its purpose. It is like the sharpening of a dull knife which requires the resistance of the grinding wheel to give it its edge. There can be no creation at all if force does not overcome the opposition of resistance! That is the lesson that has been learned by men of character and achievement, who are keenly aware that growth and power came to them only because they met the counter force of obstacles with their own dynamic energy and emerged from the ordeal greatly strengthened and triumphant. An example of this type of force working away at an obstacle until it finally conquered it is the proverbial Joshua's blast from his horn which tore down the walls of Jericho, or the sight of a youngster in a school gymnasium learning how to pick up a hundred pound weight by first lifting a twenty-five pound, then a fifty pound, then a seventy-five pound weight until he has built up enough energy and stamina to tackle the job he wanted to do in the first place which was the lifting of the hundred pound weight itself. This is a simple example of the use of intelligence directing energy to overcome the seemingly unachievable.

Purpose can never be achieved by standing still or sitting at ease in one's home. Intelligence as we have just observed overcomes obstacles. It does this through the process of solving problems through thought or thinking. Thinking is an interesting process. It takes place in the mind of course, and is evident subjectively through the projection of mental pictures, images, or ideas which flash through the mind, and are transposed to others through the use of words.

For example we are confronted with a problem. Images, mental pictures, and ideas flash in our minds in a manner calculated to test the problem in a trial and error manner before we act it out in actual fact. This activity goes on in the mind and is a process by which solutions are obtained. This is intelligence and thinking at work something that only human beings can do. The whole problem is pre-tested, as it were, and there given actual form and reality in time and space through the use of words and the creation of objects. Notice we have used symbols which were not the physical things themselves but signs of them, and these signs or ideas have made it possible for us to deal with things in our brains even though we may have been far away from the things we were thinking about. These signs or symbols, or ideas, or images make it possible for us to view the future or to review the past in our mind's eye through the phenomenon of thought. It is a sort of miracle isn't it? Now while it is true that all persons do not have the same mental capacity to think, or to make similar use of the intellectual tools like abstract ideas and images, we are all capable of understanding and using simple ideas, unless we are mentally deficient, and since most us are not, we will not concern ourselves with those categories of sub-normal mentalities that are unable to make proper use of these symbols. On the other hand, there are those like philosophers, scientists, and mathematicians who work with the highest forms of symbols and abstractions that are way over the head of average people like ourselves. We are not, in this volume, interested in them either. This writing has been prepared for average every day people with average every day problems, and that of course includes most of us.

We are now coming to grips with the basic purpose of this book which revolves, as we now know, around the use of both the conscious and subconscious minds and the manipulating of ideas. The title of the book clearly illustrates that we are suggesting two techniques of attaining greater mental power and ease of mind. I trust that I have demonstrated up to this point that we have in our power to improve ourselves if we properly apply the use of intelligence. I have spoken of tension; its causes and effects, and of happiness and its conditions and goals. I want now to get down to discussing the practical aspects of our problem which is in this instance the first of our two techniques of achieving mental and spiritual power.

We first start with the individual. How can he determine what he can achieve? How can he create a moral and ideal personality? He obviously can do neither of these unless he takes stock of himself. He must become aware of his strength and his weakness, and must expand and strengthen the former while he diminishes or completely eliminates the latter. He must set a goal for himself. That goal must be the ideal to which he himself aspires, and he must follow that path unswervingly after he has selected his purpose. As Charles Wendt once declared, "Success in life is a matter not so much of talent or opportunity as of concentration and perseverance." This goal cannot be achieved ideally or in a simple manner. The use of energy overcoming the opposing force will operate for him, as it operates for everything in the universe, if he is strong enough, and our technique will, we think, make him so strong that he can overwhelm all obstacles that lie in the path of his achievement. This victory over himself and his environment will give him moral and mental joys that he has never known before! As his personality becomes better integrated and consequently more forceful he will have become better able to dominate his environment and to form and use it to his heart's desire. It will seem like something of a miracle, but that will appear so only on the surface, for the miracle is at bottom a sincere striving for development, and is in fact, the final act in the drama of great personal concentration and effort. The fully developed personality who has achieved this high estate through patience, intelligence, self-reliance, and self-control, knows as no one else can know the keen pleasure that comes from the attainment of maturity. He is the stuff that leaders are made of, and the foundation upon which progress and society is built. His attitude toward life is that of self-reliance, both in his personal and social responsibilities. He solves his own problems because he is able to, and because he knows that the solution of these problems makes him a stronger and better person. His self-reliance is habitual and is the outgrowth of repeated successes that have created a triumphant feeling of self-confidence in his abilities. He is the mature, happy, and proud man who is strong without being pretentious, the ideal man! The man of force and substance!

Our technique of controlled relaxation can only be made effective through the use of such phenomena as the power of suggestion, which is vitally important as a source of growth and creativity; meditation, which is the awareness of both the conscious and subconscious minds, and ideas which are the medium through which our recordings pierce the conscious mind, and enter into the sleeping realm of the subconscious, where the hidden powers of psychic energy are waiting to be released.

In Harper's dictionary, we find that the word suggestion means: To place or bring an idea, proposition, etc., before a person's mind for consideration or possible action. It further says in a psychological sense: That it is the process of accepting a proposition for belief or action in the absence of the intervening and critical thought that would normally occur. This definition admirably serves our purpose because our technique of controlled relaxation has as its purpose the achievement of the precise condition made clear in the definition of the word: suggestion. Our technique has its effect through the force of suggestion which is directed at the individual who reclines in a relaxed position or as we say in a condition of "Controlled Relaxation." We will discuss this more fully later in this chapter.

For the moment let us discuss in passing the nature and function of the subconscious mind. As we discuss it somewhat more fully on a later page we will content ourselves for the moment with just a desultory description of it. First, of all, let us say that deeply imbedded in ourselves is the dynamism of the subconscious mind in which lies dormant the tremendously, positive side of our natures. Here lies in secret the hidden part of ourselves which has been repressed for reasons formerly known, but now forgotten. Since these repressed notions are now outside the sphere of our comprehension, we continue unaware of the potent power and desires that lie in this mechanism which are waiting to be used. In truth it is the seat of the real force and power that is to be found within us and it is waiting to be released under the proper circumstances. It is the release of this energy that makes for the greatest development and power of the individual. This subconscious mind is the actual center of our physical and psychological power, and is the repository of our repressed memories and also controls all the organic processes of the human body. It is this tremendous power plant that is galvanized into activity by the stimuli originating in our recorded suggestions which activate the subconscious mind and bring into play the tremendous force inherent in the subconscious mind. It is the release of this power that makes a new person out of a previously confused and defeated one.

To continue our discussion of suggestion it cannot be emphasized too strongly that suggestion to be truly effective must of necessity by-pass the conscious mind because that entity, acting as the censor, can prevent the suggestion from penetrating to the area of the subconscious, which it must reach, in order to release its psychic and physical powers.

Suggestions have several functions. We are not here concerned with the every day suggestions found in books, newspapers, advertising, movies and the like, but with its special use in the areas of therapy and inspiration. Its greatest value and effect is to be found in its direct appeal to the subconscious mind and its release for constructive action. In the eastern world suggestion has been used as a therapeutic agent for centuries and with astounding effect. It has also been used with marvelous results in the fields of hypnosis and auto-suggestion. These are discussed more fully in a later chapter. Since we are only immediately interested in suggestion as it can be used as inspiration and motivation in our technique we are merely mentioning these related uses casually, and are considering such material as is necessary for an understanding of our first technique of "Controlled Relaxation," and the power of its effective inspirational dynamism.

Let us now at long last proceed to the matter at hand. We have up to this moment discussed such factors as suggestion, ideas, the conscious and subconscious mind, intelligence, and other incidental phenomena that are essential to human understanding and happiness. Our discussion has been both general and in some cases specific. What we have been doing is gradually building a foundation on which to establish the activation of our first technique—that of "Controlled Relaxation." Now that we have, I believe, done this let us proceed with a detailed analysis of the means required to attain the goal of all our striving, namely, happiness, maturity, and success.

MENTAL POWER Through CONTROLLED RELAXATION

The mind can best be influenced and controlled when it is in a state of reflection or meditation. It can then be directed and mastered, but it can only be so influenced if the meditation or reflection is absolute, that is to say, it can only achieve complete introversion when the conscious release is complete and when the environment has melted away or completely disappeared from the awareness of consciousness. It is this state that is so vitally necessary and important to the function of suggestion, for it is only then that we have entered into a higher degree of self-consciousness and self-communion. This state brings with it an understanding and clarity about life and the universe that is impossible to attain under normal circumstances. In this state the person is lifted out of himself, so to speak, and becomes a part of the cosmic consciousness. He feels uplifted, inspired, more complete, and more integrated with himself and the universe than he has ever been before. He feels a joy that transcends all human understanding. In short, he is in tune with the psychic mysteries of the infinite, and discovers in himself depths he never knew he possessed.

We recommend, as part of our first technique of "Controlled Relaxation," that a condition of isolation and meditation be established. We suggest, therefore, that a period of each day be set aside for the purpose of relaxed and controlled meditation. We recommend going into a room, closing the door, shutting out all impinging and distracting sounds, lying down on a couch or bed and relaxing. We know that after lying inertly for a time the sweet balm of release will come to the reclining one. The passive body lying in delicate balance between consciousness and unconsciousness is in the best possible condition for communion with the subconscious mind, which as we have already learned is the basic source of our physical and psychic power.

It is here that our technique of "Controlled Relaxation" comes into play. Please note that we have used the words "Controlled Relaxation" not just relaxation. In our technique of "Controlled Relaxation" we recognize the dynamic power of words and ideas. We know that thought is force, as Dr. Emile Coue, the famous French psychologist, stated, and that it has the dynamic power to move and change those who are exposed to its influence under the most proper conditions. Our technique employs the use of hetero-suggestion since the ideas conveyed to the subconscious are not of the reclining one's choosing, but are those transposed to that individual through the medium of our inspirational recordings. In the final sense all suggestion is auto-suggestion, but we nevertheless recognize that since our method is one of hetero-suggestion we need not go to great lengths to mention auto-suggestion, other than to say that it is also an invaluable method in the field of suggestion, which has its source however in the consciously selected ideas of the individual acting on himself. As evidence of auto-suggestion, we are all of us aware of the remarkable inspirations that come to our gifted geniuses of the arts during their periods of contemplation or day dreaming. The auto-suggested inspirations which arose out of the inspired states of contemplation of such geniuses as Tchaikovsky, Beethoven, Dickens, and Victor Hugo, who conceived ideas and inspirations in this deep state of auto-suggestion that they could not possibly have achieved in their less inspired moments, were accomplishments of tremendous proportions. These manifestations of auto-suggestion and self-inspiration are interesting and enlightening but are outside the realm of our consideration at this time. The hetero-suggestion of our "Controlled Relaxation" has however the same effects if done under the conditions we have proposed. The same depths of power can be released through the inspiration of our recorded suggestions.

The fact that the body is in a state of relaxation is desirable, but that is not enough, if the real intention is to use these relaxed periods not only for release and forgetfulness, but for personal growth and happiness. This can only be done through the control and selection of ideas that enter into the receptive mind of the relaxed person, who under these conditions is in a highly susceptible state. This control of selected ideas is made possible through the medium of our highly charged inspirational records that are played softly and soothingly to the reclining person whose susceptibility under these conditions we have already conceded.

These inspirational recordings, we have a whole series of them, are so remarkably effective because the trancelike state of this relaxed period makes it possible for the recorded ideas and suggestions to be sent directly to the subconscious mind since the critical faculties of the usually very alert conscious mind are at such a time in a state of quiescence and thus afford no obstacle to the transference of these suggestions. This direct contact, which is not possible under any other condition, with the exception of sleep and hypnosis, creates a stimulus response cycle in the subconscious that releases powers that were hitherto unknown and untapped. With this development the new force of ideas, inspirations, ambitions, and motivations come dynamically to the surface bringing with them a new sense of strength, purpose, and well-being.

This then is the technique of "Controlled Relaxation." It is dynamic, sure, and opens splendid new horizons of power and happiness. It is a wonderful means of growth and inspiration! It is not a magical technique, but is based on the findings of psychological science!. People today are confused, nervous, frustrated, and are frantically searching for some way to resolve their troubles. Our technique of "Controlled Relaxation" not only gives them an opportunity to relax and find physical regeneration, which is important in itself, but adds to it the wholesome and inspirational expansion of their mental and spiritual powers! These inspirational, controlled, relaxation records can be used in the quiet solitude of your own home, and are therefore very simple to utilize.

MENTAL POWER Through CONTROLLED RELAXATION

Man does not live by bread alone! Happiness is not something that drops into one's mouth like a grape from a vine! It must be sought to be achieved! I can think of no better way to achieve this happiness and maturity than by opening up the vast powers of your subconscious through the recorded suggestions of our inspirational records, and putting them at your service for a happier, fuller, and longer life! Would you know the joy and beauty of life and living? Then develop yourself to your fullest capacity as a human being so that you can truly enjoy the splendours of the universe!

You can make your own phonograph records if you desire or use a tape recorder for this purpose, which is also an excellent means of conveying suggestions to the subconscious. For those of you who are interested in the "Mental Power Records" write directly to me, and I shall be glad to send you a catalogue of my latest records. Write to: Melvin Powers, 12015 Sherman Road, No. Hollywood, California 91605.

CHAPTER IV

The Subconscious Mind in Action

"Mind Moves Matter." Vergil.

Now THAT WE have finished discussing the first of our two techniques and demonstrated how this technique can open up infinite horizons of mental and spiritual power, we will proceed to a preoccupation with the second one, which is also an amazing new method of influencing the mind through the potent medium of suggestion, which has been mentioned but sketchily in the third chapter, and which will be treated much more substantially as we proceed. This new and amazing method is called "Sleep Suggestion." We are going to devote the rest of the book to an analysis and discussion of this new method of achieving mental and spiritual development. We will illustrate how this is done through the communication of recorded suggestions to the sleeper. It is necessary to note that while in the first technique the individual is given suggestions during a deep state of relaxation or meditation in the second he is exposed to suggestion while in the state of slumber. Let us now proceed with our "Sleep Suggestion" technique.

MENTAL-POWER THROUGH SLEEP-SUGGESTION

To continue what has only been slightly suggested in chapter three let us enter into a fuller discussion of the conscious and subconscious minds. As I have already pointed out in discussing our first technique of "Controlled Relaxation" we have two minds, the conscious and the subconscious. Each is endowed with separate and distinct functions and powers, and under certain conditions each works independently of the other. It is the conscious mind that is the source of thinking and it is that mind which we use in our daily problems which require rational behavior. Its chief activity is that of reason, and its chief business that of making it possible for us to function in the every day world through the cooperation of the five senses.

The subconscious mind on the other hand has a more complex and subtle function and is rooted in instinct. Its purpose is to maintain the security of the human being through meeting the needs of the body under normal and abnormal conditions. Another one of its functions is to preserve the life of the individual under conditions of emergency. Still another is to operate in the area of the psychic realm through the use of its strange and psychic powers which make it possible for the individual to think, feel, and contact outer and inner forces that are unavailable to the conscious mind. It is in this inter-relationship between the conscious and subconscious minds that the source of our mental, emotional, and spiritual power lies. This power can only be released if there is a forceful and powerful conscious will to generate it through positive and constructive motivation.

THE SUBCONSCIOUS MIND IN ACTION

The conscious mind is like the part of the tree that is above the soil while the top roots can be likened to the subconscious from which the tree gains its strength. The subconscious mind in action is a remarkable instrument. For example, it is time to go to bed. The alarm clock, which had worked only too efficiently this morning will not run for some inexplicable reason. What to do? It is eleven thirty o'clock, all the stores are closed. Can't stay up all night to avoid being late to work the next morning. Just a moment! There is a solution to the problem! It has been done by many people who never heard of or saw an alarm clock, or ever dreamed there was such fancy concepts as the subconscious mind or the power of suggestion. That's it! A self-suggestion to get up at a certain time in the morning. It's done. The thought is implanted in the mind. It slides into the subconscious and lo and behold morning comes and out of bed jumps the sleeper who has not only gotten up on time, but has performed an experiment in which the power of self-suggestion, and the role of the subconscious mind have made their important contributions.

The subconscious never sleeps. The foregoing experience was a good example of this type of activity which is automatic and never ending. The ideas or suggestions that we have on our minds as we fall asleep are the springboard for whatever dreams or thoughts we experience during the long night of slumber. Many of us, for example, have gone to sleep with problems on our minds and to our surprise have found that we had worked them out during the night through the use of our subconscious minds. A composer, for instance, had informed me that he had had difficulty composing a theme for one of his songs until a chance remark he heard before going to bed one night proved sufficiently inspirational to get him up in the middle of the night to put his "dream song" on paper, and a beautiful song it was, too, for he played it to me soon after that creative experience. This is another excellent example of the power of suggestion and the subconscious.

I have already suggested, note the word, that the subconscious mind is involuntary in action. It is this mind that controls us during the hours of our slumber. We may roll to the edge of the bed without falling out of it because we are protected from doing so by the ever vigilant subconscious. We also may become uncovered during the night and find that condition is corrected without our need of waking because the subconscious registers the fact, and tends to the matter automatically without causing us to interrupt our slumber. In passing, it is necessary to remember in any consideration of the subconscious mind that it controls the functions of our organs, that it is automatic, and that it is preeminently susceptible to the force of suggestions. With these facts firmly settled in our minds, we can go on to the next phase of the wonders of the subconscious mind in action. We have discussed suggestion as it is used in

THE SUBCONSCIOUS MIND IN ACTION

the waking hours, now let us concern ourselves with the problem of sleep suggestion, that is a suggestion which is relayed to a sleeping individual. It is with this phase of suggestion that we will be preoccupied hereafter.

Dr. Emile Coue, the famous French psychologist, was interested in and an advocate of the use of sleep suggestion. He confined his practice to this field and to the area of child psychology. We see no reason why sleep suggestion cannot be used with admirable effect on adults as well since the conditions of susceptibility are equivalent in both cases.

The hours of sleep are an excellent time for the application of suggestion. Almost all books on hypnotism speak of the transformation of normal sleep into hypnotic sleep through the transmission of suggestions to the sleeper. This has not always been practicable in the past because of the sleeper's resistance to the possibility of divulging ideas and thoughts that were of a confidential nature. This problem has now, however, been solved by the introduction of the sleep-o-matic units which we will discuss at greater length in the later stages of this book.

Let us pursue this matter of sleep suggestion a bit further. I will narrate a couple of experiences that will graphically demonstrate the phenomenon of sleep suggestion in its simplest form.

I was reading a story to a friend of mine one evening, and while I was doing so, she fell asleep. I wasn't at all aware of this until I had read several pages. Noticing that she was asleep I decided to try an experiment. I woke her and questioned her as to the content of my reading. She recalled nothing. I then put her under hypnosis. While in that condition she was able to repeat verbatim what I had read to her. Before bringing her back to the normal state I suggested that she would remember consciously everything that she repeated to me while under hypnosis. I woke her and she then proceeded consciously to repeat the pages to me. Extremely interesting, wasn't it? The identical experience can be duplicated through the use of recordings which changes normal sleep into hypnotic sleep, and then back to normal sleep again. The heightened receptivity of the mind, plus the use of post-hypnotic suggestions make the process easier and more effective.

At another time, I visited a friend only to be informed by his daughter that he was asleep. I again decided to try an experiment. I gave him a suggestion as he lay there in deep slumber. I told him slowly and clearly that when he awakened, I was going to ask him how far Los Angeles was from San Francisco, and that he was going to tell me that it was 1,324 miles away. I thereupon left the room, but not before instructing his wife that she was to wake him within the hour. We settled down to wait for his appearance. He came in with his usual warm greeting, for we were the best of friends, and after he had sat for a while I casually asked

THE SUBCONSCIOUS MIND IN ACTION

him whether he knew how far it was to San Francisco. He looked at me rather surprised at such a question and said that of course he knew. It was 1,324 miles. "Anybody knows that," he declared. With this we all burst into hearty laughter and then I proceeded to explain our little experiment. He remained skeptical insisting that it was in fact 1,324 miles. He persisted in his contention until we produced a paper we had prepared stating the exact situation and how he would react to it. He noticed 1,324 miles on the paper, hurried to get a road map, observing it closely, noticed that the distance was only 405 miles. He looked at each of us sheepishly and burst into thunderous laughter as he finally appreciated the full humor of the situation.

Should you decide to try this experiment keep the following points in mind: Attract the attention of the sleeper and give him suggestions that he will remember everything after he awakens. The suggestions should be worded something as follows:

"Do not awaken when you hear my voice. . . . Continue to sleep deeply. . . . Do not awaken. Your sleep is becoming deeper and deeper. . . . You are now sleeping deeply, however you can hear my voice and you will remember everything that I am about to say to you. . . . You will remember everything that I say. . . . . (Give the sleeper whatever material you desire at this time.) . . . When you awaken, you will feel very refreshed, healthy, and happy."

MENTAL-POWER THROUGH SLEEP-SUGGESTION

This experiment vividly demonstrates the magic of sleep suggestion. It must have become clearer to the reader by this time after the iteration and re-iteration of the word suggestion that it does wield a very powerful influence on us, both in our thoughts and in society. For what is advertising and the art of propaganda if not an intense application of the principles of suggestion? It is therefore incumbent upon ourselves if we wish to become healthy and happy people to use this force of suggestion in a manner best calculated to make us think more positively and constructively so that we can become more complete and successful human beings. This is not an easy matter! Conscious barriers must be washed away, and access to the subconscious mind must be made possible through the effective use of sleep suggestion. The instruments through which this can be attained are the sleep-o-matic units which transmit suggestions, in such a manner and under such conditions, as to make access to the subconscious a certainty.

CHAPTER V

The Power of Suggestion

"Give Me a Lever Long Enough and Prop Strong Enough, I Can Single Handed Move the World." Archimedes.

THE THEORY of suggestion was first elaborated on by Dr. James Braid (1795-1860), an English physician. There is no doubt today that this theory has gained added weight through its importance as a medium in inducing hypnosis. There are two types of suggestion, the direct and indirect forms. I shall enlarge upon this more fully later in this chapter. The direct type of suggestion is positive and instigates action. The negative or indirect type inhibits action by confusing consciousness or masking the communication so that its true purposes is not understood by the respondent.

Although Braid elaborated on his theory of suggestion on a more scientific scale, suggestion itself and auto-suggestion go back to the ancient Hindus. They employed auto-suggestion as a means of achieving moral perfection. This use of auto-suggestion, which is the deliberate influencing of one's self through the use of mental pictures, spread to Chaldea, Mesopotamia, Syria, Egypt, and into Greece where it was taught by the Greek philosophers. It thereafter was transmitted to the Latin moralists. In the latter part of the nineteenth century, Dr. Croste de Lagrave and Dr. Emile Coue, did much to advance knowledge in this field both in auto and mass suggestion. These were forerunners to the scientific findings of Dr. Braid, who more than any of his predecessors, stressed the psychological nature of hypnosis.

Susceptibility to suggestion is present during the hours that we are awake. It is, however, modified and weakened, or diverted by the obstructions of reason, lack of attention, and the interference of judgment. During the period of sleep these mechanisms are weakened, while the imagination takes on greater strength. Impressions are accepted without question and are transformed into images, sensations, action, and movements. This state being more tractable permits the subconscious to gain easier access to transmitted suggestions and influences. This is the basic factor that makes sleep suggestion so effective in mental therapy.

THE POWER OF SUGGESTION

You will recall that I stated in my book, "Hypnotism Revealed," that all hypnotism is self-hypnosis. I had also stated that increased susceptibility is the main characteristic of the hypnotic state. I had further pointed out that normal sleep can be converted into a sleep suggestion state through the use of the sleep-o-matic units.

The cure of warts by suggestion is well-known. The proof that suggestive treatment can be efficacious in functional and non-functional diseases was a discovery of considerable importance. To treat an ulcer, it is necessary not only to treat the physical aspects of the organism, but the mental as well.

Suggestion is an idea which undergoes transformation into an action.

The task before us now is to make good use of suggestion, considering it as one of the natural forces, and looking upon it as an instrument for gaining self-mastery. Sleep suggestions are just as powerful as suggestions given under hypnosis.

There is a psychological condition that is prerequisite to all suggestion. There must be the genuine desire on the part of the individual to attain the goal that he has outlined for himself. It is this intensity of purpose that acts as the catalyst in the achievement of this goal.

MENTAL-POWER THROUGH SLEEP-SUGGESTION

Let us at this time further investigate this matter of suggestion. In the literature on suggestion, reference is made to prestige suggestion, non-prestige suggestion, waking suggestion, and hypnotic suggestion. Prestige suggestions are those in which the suggestions are given in a direct form by another person or by a mechanical means such as a phonograph or a tape-recorder which are our two types of sleep-o-matic units. It is with this type of suggestion that we are primarily concerned. Suggestions like you are going to sleep; your eyes are closing, and you are going to be hypnotized are typical examples of direct suggestion. These suggestions may be given in either the waking or hypnotic state. The distinction between waking suggestions and hypnotic suggestions is an artificial one however, since in fact all suggestions are administered actually in a waking state, or the subject would not respond to them. This is true in a basic sense even though one subject might be awake while another is in a state of deep sleep. It is, however, the sleep state that is more amenable to suggestion because of the relaxed and highly susceptible condition of the sleeper, a fact that we hope we have already firmly established.

THE POWER OF SUGGESTION

The following article which appeared in the May 28, 1951 edition of Newsweek, is an example of prestige or direct suggestions.

BRAVE NEW RECORDINGS

"I can rid myself of any symptoms, completely and in less than a minute," drones the loudspeaker. "I'm not overly dependent on medicine or on doctors," the confident voice continues. Then in a monotone, over and over: "My mind is a blank. I am relaxing . . . relaxing . . ."

By amplified tape recordings, recitations of this kind in otherwise quiet hospital wards are now relieving the "terror dreams" of mentally ill war veterans. Within three to four weeks of the "suggestion" treatment, which follows the simple principles of hypnosis (and some imaginative scenes from Aldous Huxley's "Brave New World"), most patients report gratifying results. Dr. Ernst Schmidhofer of Kennedy Veterans Hospital, Memphis, Tenn., told his colleagues at the American Psychiatric Association meeting in Cincinnati, of the success of this new technique which is being applied at his institution.

Some of the men are able for the first time in their lives to nap in the daytime. Sleep is more quiet and refreshing. Patients dream less or have pleasant dreams instead of nightmares. Almost no one except newly admitted men ask for sleeping pills. Dr. Schmidhofer added that there is "much less arising to smoke and to pace about restlessly."

Patients at Kennedy Veterans Hospital get the "sleep program" every night from 10 p.m. to 7 a.m. There is a much shorter daytime treatment. The loudspeakers are in the ward and the recorder in the nurse's office. Dr. Schmidhofer recommends the use of this method to bring much-needed restful sleep and relaxation to patients suffering from all types of mental illness, psychosomatic ailments, and pains of various sorts.

MENTAL-POWER THROUGH SLEEP-SUGGESTION

There is another type of hypnotic suggestion that I haven't as yet discussed, and that is the post-hypnotic variety. Such suggestions are given during the hypnotic state, and are to be carried out in the normal state upon a previously arranged signal or a set time. The variety of post-hypnotic acts that will be performed are limited only by the suggestions given. If the subject is told that he will go to the store and buy a magazine in an hour, he will carry out the suggestions explicitly. The post-hypnotic suggestions are therefore similar to the waking ones that will be carried out at a later time.

It becomes quite apparent that suggestions, of whatever variety, are a tremendous force. Doesn't it? One of our main purposes in preparing this book was to show you, the reader, the incredible power of suggestion, and to show you the way to use your latent power through this wonderful vital means of motivation. In order for suggestion of any kind to take effect, it behooves the individual to sincerely desire to achieve his ends, and to remember that this desire is the basic force that makes self-mastery and development possible.

Many renowned healers of the past effected cures through the skillful use of suggestion after orthodox methods had failed. They may have used illogical and fantastic means, but they nevertheless effected miraculous cures because they were adept in the art of manipu-

lating the suggestible pre-dispositions of
The successes of the healers were also in la
to their own self-confidence which was con
their patients so effectively that they were half   .ed
before the treatment began. Such is the beneficent influence of positive suggestion!

The discovery that suggestion was instrumental in bringing about cures both in functional and non-functional ailments was a discovery of the greatest importance. We are today aware of the reciprocal action between the mind and body. Psycho-somatic medicine is based on this correlation. We all know, for instance, the physical symptoms of fear. The face becomes pale, the legs refuse to function, the heart begins to beat violently, we perspire profusely, and our thoughts become confused. Why does this happen? It happens because every idea has a corresponding physical reaction and because ideas or suggestions strongly effect our bodies. This gives us an opportunity to observe how the force of ideas or suggestions control our bodily actions and reactions, both in the conscious and subconscious realms.

Habits of mind and body are created through constant repetition. Since the strength of our personalities is based on our attitudes and habits, it is important that we carefully condition ourselves for the best possible utilization of our potentials. This can be done only through the most constant attention to our mental and physical patterns which can make or break us as the saying goes.

A positive frame of mind based on constructive mental attitudes can be brought about by proper suggestion so that such desirable characteristics as cleanliness, determination, modesty, confidence, and courage become regular features of an individual's behavior. It is best, of course, if these characteristics are cultivated during the greater plasticity of childhood. If they are not, proper suggestions can do their work in later years. We know today that when an idea or goal is coupled with a powerful emotion or drive the chances for success become greater. It is necessary for us, therefore, to make a conscious effort to control our thoughts so that we will not be hampered in our attempts to attain positive, constructive goals.

It is amazing how an idea or a suggestion seems to be transformed into reality! Have you at one time or another expected a call and heard what you thought was the phone ringing only to find you had imagined it? It seemed to be the real thing didn't it, but it was only a self-induced illusion! The power of the mind is strange indeed! Medical students become at times so deeply engrossed in the study of disease that they sometimes

THE POWER OF SUGGESTION

exhibit the symptoms of those maladies they are studying even though their conditions are perfectly normal. How about the inveterate dispenser of falsehoods? He lies so convincingly that he ofttimes believes his own falsehoods. Ideas are powerful indeed! You think of your favorite food, your mouth waters. You think of a crayon being used scratchingly across the blackboard, it sets you on edge. You think that some part of your body is itching, and you immediately feel the sensation, or you see someone yawn, and that suggestion is sufficiently strong to set you off doing the same.

Tremendous powers are inherent in ideas, thoughts, and suggestions. Through the power of suggestion the blind have been known to see, while the lame have been inspired to walk! We sophisticates are perhaps above carrying charms, good luck pieces, four leaf clovers, rabbits feet, and such trinkets. These are undoubtedly irrational safeguards, but they are of great interest to us as students of the literature of suggestion because they illustrate our point that suggestion can be used in many ways. In this instance these good luck symbols suggest security and good fortune, and even though they have no intrinsic value in themselves, they do give those that believe in their potency a sense of power that would otherwise be lacking.

MENTAL-POWER THROUGH SLEEP-SUGGESTION

The late Austrian novelist and playwrite, Arthur Schnitzler, called the human mind the "Vast Domain." We too are struck with the manifold wonder of its subtlety and power! We too feel that it is an instrument that can accomplish miracles once it is prepared to do so!

In closing our discussion on suggestion, it is important to note that it has three component phases: The idea, the unconscious working of the idea, and the end product which is the result. A suggestion can, in fact, enter our conscious minds without conscious effort on our part, and sometimes even in the defiance of our willpower thus producing unpleasant subconscious effects. This condition can cause such difficulty as to require the attention of psychotherapy. If it does, the healing power of positive suggestions can be used as a means of bringing the individual back to his original healthy state of mind.

I have written a new book dealing with the subject of dynamic thinking. This book will show you how you can effectively use the power contained within your subconscious mind for achieving self-confidence and success. The book is titled, "Dynamic Thinking" and sells for one dollar. It is further described on the back cover of this book. I highly recommend the book for your further reading and understanding of the power of suggestion.

CHAPTER VI

Mental-Therapy Through Sleep Suggestion

"Sleep Is the Best Cure for Waking Troubles." Cervantes

SLEEP COMES to us after the stress and strain of the day's activity has taken its toll of our energies. We seek peace and relaxation, and the regeneration of our tired brains and bodies. We slumber, we dream, but interestingly enough while our brain finds surcease from the cares of the day, the mind remains alive, active, and constantly alert to impressions, both new and old. It is this subconscious mind that is the main object of our interest. It is this subconscious mind that is in contact with the deepest recesses of our beings. It is attuned not only to our innermost selves but to the subtle mysteries of the universe and our own hidden power. It is able to send out and receive messages and lives a life of its own while the rest of us lies in the deepest oblivion. This is the instrument that is the wonder and the mystery to those probers of the human mind—the mental therapist!

The scientific knowledge of the subconscious mind is rather a recent discovery. We have already discussed this more fully on a previous page. We cannot say, and certainly, Dr. Sigmund Freud, the father of psychoanalysis, never intended to say, nor did he ever maintain, that the subconscious is a tangible part of the human body or mind. He made its dynamism known to us, and noted its unique function and tremendous power. It is with that wonderful power that we are pre-occupied, rather than with the consideration of its physical make up.

The subconscious mind is in control during the period of sleep. The conscious mind having been lulled to sleep no longer serves as a barrier to the subconscious. Impressions therefore make their way quickly and unerringly to the subconscious mechanism by way of the brain. It is this clear channel that gives suggestion the added power that it has during the sleep state. I do not mean to convey the impression that the brain is not capable of being contacted, far from it. It certainly is, for how else could we convey suggestion to the sleeper? What I am trying to establish is the fact the brain being rid of the active complexity of day to day problems is less inhibited and tense in its operation, and is therefore in a greater state of receptivity. The period of sleep then obviously becomes the best time for learning and healing therapy for the reasons previously stated.

The subconscious mind does not register suggestions, thoughts or ideas discriminatingly. It accepts everything

MENTAL-THERAPY THROUGH SLEEP-SUGGESTION

that is communicated to it. The conscious mind, on the other hand, is constantly in a process of selection and rejection and does so in a relatively objective manner. This is an extremely important point to remember because the subconscious by its very nature must be protected from becoming the repository of negative and destructives ideas and suggestions, since it accepts all messages directed to it. That is what makes sleep suggestion and sleep therapy so effective a means of healing, since only constructive suggestions of beneficial and positive nature need be transmitted to the sleeper. Such a selection could hardly occur during the confusion and tension of the busy day when many psychological blocks function to eliminate an easy acceptance of positive suggestions.

We, as people, are primarily a mechanism for response and action. By means of response we try to adapt the environment to ourselves, or try to adapt ourselves to the environment. This is done through the processes of perception and thought. All mental activity leaves its traces (brain records) in the neural system. These traces or records are called neurograms, in which the memories of past experiences are stored. When these neurograms are again activated by a physiological or psychological process or state, the previous condition or action, whatever the nature of it might have been, repeats itself. Thus in a therapeutic sense if we offer suggestions of a constructive nature so that new brain traces can be built up, we are creating new neural patterns that can be reinforced through repetition. In this manner, new strength and force can be created in a person who had previously been a weak and vacillating individual.

There are several methods of contacting the subconscious mind during the sleep state. We have already established the fact that suggestion is most effective during this period because the brain, or conscious mind is in a state of passive existence and therefore does not impede access to the subconscious mind. Sleep suggestion therefore, in our opinion, is one of the best means of therapeutic healing not only because of the admirable simplicity of its methods, but since the emotions and the will are held in suspension during the sleep state, they cannot serve as road blocks on the path of rapport between the suggestion and its recipient, the sleeper. The subconscious can also be reached through the use of drugs and hypnotism. We have however already established our conviction that sleep-mental-therapy can be best achieved through the use of suggestion, a simple and efficient medium.

We are all suggestible. It is one of the characteristics of all human beings. Transmitted suggestion is in no way a violation of the subject's individuality. It is, in fact, a remarkable means of tapping the unused psychic power of the unconscious so that he can become a more

MENTAL-THERAPY THROUGH SLEEP-SUGGESTION

harmonious human being. Sleep suggestion can be exercised methodically. We have, in fact, solved this problem through the use of our sleep-o-matic units which can be used as desired or needed during the course of a night's sleep. Countless unwanted suggestions are conveyed to us during the day. We are now able to select only those suggestions we want through the use of the aforementioned sleep-o-matic units. These units also make therapy possible through the direct contact with the subconscious mind, which as I have already stated on several occasions, is the storehouse of our psychic and emotional power. Here courage, strength, health, success, and ambition can be nourished through the release of subconscious powers just as surely as the leaves of a tree turn toward the sun for their sustenance.

Sleep suggestion is a simple process. It is most easy to achieve with children because they are accustomed to having some one in authority close to them when they are preparing to go to bed, but it can work equally as well with adults when they are in a state of sound sleep. Dr. Emile Coue, of whom we have spoken previously, recommended that parents make use of the following technique:

"As soon as the child has gone to sleep, one of the parents goes very quietly into the bedroom and up to the bed. A hand is slowly and gently laid on the child's forehead. Should the child stir, and seem about to awaken, the parent says in a low tone, 'Sleep, go on sleeping, sleep soundly,' repeating the phrases until the child is sound asleep once more. Then the parent, still in the same slow and quiet tones, reiterates all the improvements desirable in the child, whether from the point of view of health, sleep, work, application, conduct, or the like. When this has been done, the parent withdraws, still taking the utmost care not to awaken the child."

This same technique can, of course, be used with phonograph records or tape recordings for both children and adults.

There is scarcely a functional disturbance of any kind that can not be helped through hypnotic suggestion, which is a heightened form of suggestion. Many therapists have long lists of patients that have been cured in this manner. Cases of psychosomatic symptoms and psychological aberrations have been cured through the means of direct suggestion.

It is generally conceded by those who are in the therapeutic field that the accumulation of excessive weight may be a symptom of a psychological disorder. The following article which appeared in the June 18, 1950 issue of the Los Angeles Times. This is evidence of the effectiveness of suggestion as used in the sleep state:

MENTAL-THERAPY THROUGH SLEEP-SUGGESTION

MENTAL SUGGESTION MAY HELP FAT-REDUCING DIET

By Lydia Lane

"Don't let people get away with the excuse that glandular trouble causes their being fat," declares a university doctor and professor, "because 99.44% of them are fat because they eat too much."

The obesity, he explained, was caused for the most part by an over-emphasis on starchy foods. But why do people overeat? Psychiatrists tell us that an abnormal appetite does not necessarily imply an excessive love of food but often is the result of emotional disturbance. What to do about this craving for food, especially in those who are not happy, becomes a real problem.

Group Effort Suggested

A solution suggested by a recent Public Health conference was the formation of a reducing group known as "Appetites Anonymous" to be patterned after the famous "Alcoholics Anonymous."

When overeating is a habit of long standing, it becomes increasingly difficult to diet. The desire to be thin is not as great as the desire to eat, so these poor unfortunates start reducing but soon break their resolutions.

Record Devised

An interesting and effective way to solve this problem is to receive constructive suggestion during sleep. There is a machine especially designed with a pillow speaker to train the subconscious mind at night.

This painless method re-educates and reconditions habits so that after sleeping over a record which suggests that you no longer have an abnormal appetite, you find yourself with unbelievable power to resist what at one time seemed irresistible.

Action Intermittent

This machine plays records which train your subconscious mind during sleep and is constructed so that it will go on and off at specified intervals.

If you have a problem of insomnia, nervousness or reducing and would like to try this method, it is possible to rent a machine at a nominal figure.

MENTAL-POWER THROUGH SLEEP-SUGGESTION

Since the state of anesthesia is a form of sleep, we feel free in inserting a recent newspaper article which demonstrates the effects of music on the conscious and subconscious during the course of surgical operations:

SURGICAL PATIENTS SOOTHED BY MUSIC
Serenading Combined With Anesthesia at University of Chicago Medical Clinics

CHICAGO, June 17.—What will you have for your operation tomorrow—classical, semiclassical or popular music?

This is a routine question anesthetists ask surgical patients at the University of Chicago medical clinics. The serenading is combined with anesthesia. It's a method of soothing the sick while they undergo surgery.

The music with anesthesia, surgeons said, relaxes the patients mentally and gives the surgical staff additional freedom to talk while working.

Rooms Equipped

The music-with-surgery program was expanded when the Nathan Goldblatt Memorial Hospital on the campus opened this week. The hospital specializes in cancer research. Its six major operating rooms and six preparation rooms for surgery are equipped with music dispensing facilities.

The surgical patient hears the music he likes. Beethoven, Victor Herbert or Perry Como selections are available for adult patients. Children are offered tunes from "Cinderella," "Peter and the Wolf," "Pinocchio" and other favorites.

The music is piped to the operating room from a central recorder room. Two channels of musical recordings are placed on a narrow strip of magnetic tape. Each of the three recorder units will play four hours of continuous music.

Patients hear music in the room where they are prepared for surgery. The music of their choice is heard from a mounted wall speaker. The soft music reduces the tension and allows the anesthetist to converse with the patient during the administration of the anesthetic.

MENTAL-THERAPY THROUGH SLEEP-SUGGESTION

Through Earphones

Light weight stethoscope-type earphones are fitted to the patient in the surgery room. Only the patient and the anesthetist hear the music as the surgeon works.

The practice of furnishing music for surgery, however, is not a new idea. It is as old as Egypt. The Pharaohs' physicians chanted while treating the sick. In the Middle Ages, groups of singers were employed to soothe the ill during epidemics.

It is called "music for surgery." The work is headed by Dr. Lester R. Dragstedt, chairman of the department of surgery of the university's clinical center.

Surgeons have reported on the success of using the phonograph and radio in the operating room. A study of 10 patients hearing the "surgical sonatas" was made at the University of Chicago medical clinics. The anesthetists found less emotional disturbance when music was used.

The idea of providing music during surgery was first tested at the clinics in 1947. It was a research experiment to help lessen tensions of patients undergoing major surgery. It is used with spinal, local or regional anesthesia.

Results with music were determined by the reaction of the patients and by the quantity of anesthetic agents employed.

The word suggestion requires one explantion in its usage. It is essential that the mode of suggestion should be adapted to the individual needs of the passive agent. In some cases the suggestion of a simple word is all that is needed in establishing an impression favorable to the subject; in others it might be necessary to use logic, to affirm strongly, to convince; in others, to use the gentle persuasion of insinuation. Our sleep-o-matic phonograph records and tape recorder tapes take into consideration all of these factors.

CHAPTER VII

Memory Development While You Sleep

"Memory Is the Treasury and Guardian of All Things." Cicero

It IS SURPRISING INDEED that many people do not realize the importance of memory. To a large extent we are what our experiences have made us. What value is there in experience if it is not registered in our brain in a manner that can be useful in the future? Imagine not being able to recall anything we have read, learned, or seen! It would be like coming out of the vacuum of yesterday and going into the void of tomorrow. Without the memory there is no learning! Without learning there can be no development of the personality or any assurance of success! If our memories are faulty we retain little, whereas a strong memory assures maximum capability and development. If we are able to retain more and learn more rapidly, greater efficiency is assured. If the memory is weak, that is to say undeveloped, it can be trained to become stronger just as a weak leg can be restored to supple strength through the proper exercises.

The training of the memory is not a new idea. The Greeks placed great value on a well developed memory and created a system in which association was used as the basis for memory improvement. Memory courses based on Aristotle's concept of association were taught to the young aristrocrats of Greece. The Romans later took over the Greek system of memory training and used it to great advantage in learning and speaking. The difficulty with this was that those who were admitted into the secrets of the methods of memory training were sworn not to divulge this very esoteric science to any one. The few who were granted this privilege were the intellectual leaders of their day. The masses, on the other hand, were considered neither good nor important enough to learn the secrets of memory. We today, of course, with our democratic heritage, have other ideas on this subject. It is my private opinion that included in every educational program, time and opportunity should be set aside for memory development. What studies, after all, can one understand and retain without a good memory?

A Good Memory is a Lifelong Asset

What did you forget to do today? Can you remember what day it was last week that you meant to telephone someone, purchase some article, or write someone, but that it had somehow slipped your mind? How many times have you said, "I forgot." How many times have you said, "Your name is on the tip of my tongue, but I just can't remember it." How many times have you been embarrassed because you couldn't remember a person's name?

MENTAL-POWER THROUGH SLEEP-SUGGESTION

Too many people have a tendency to complain of their faulty memory without doing anything to improve it. They look upon a poor memory as a handicap which must be borne and which they feel cannot be improved. Yet, the rapid improvement after using one of our sleep-o-matic units is as startling as it is rewarding. A poor memory is more than a mere annoyance. It is a serious handicap, but one which can with proper guidance and intelligent effort be corrected.

The inability to recall is not necessarily attributable to a faulty memory but rather a failure to retain the name or material to be remembered. In other words, the pictures and associations made on the brain were blurred, indistinct, and foggy. This is reflected in the inability to remember names, faces, facts, and figures. It is actually the failure of the brain mechanism to register and picture the names or material adequately.

Memory In Business and Salesmanship

A good memory is priceless in business as well as in social activities. An accurate, retentive memory may be the basis for business success. Without it, one may fail despite one's educational background. The business world pays the largest salaries to men with the best equipped minds. Develop your memory and be the exceptional man.

A successful sales talk requires a "skilled memory." A salesman is greatly dependent upon it. However, he frequently thinks of excellent sales points after he has left his prospect when it is of course too late. In all lines of business, the salesman must be fully conversant with all sales information and statistical data. Inability to retain these has caused failure.

You Can Remember Names and Faces

Many people may suffer financially because of their inability to remember names and faces. A doctor, for instance, who perhaps fails to remember the patient's name on the second visit may lose him because the patient interprets the doctor's poor memory as an indication of his lack of interest in his welfare. The same condition can prevail for any profession or business. The patient, client or customer's reaction is not unreasonable since his name should have been remembered.

Improving the memory does not mean burdening it. Actually there is no limit to its capacity. The use and exercise of the memory will make it easier for you to retain impressions. It is like a storehouse which has unlimited capacity. You need not accept a poor memory as inevitable. You can develop its power.

Memory In Education

Education is limited entirely by the capacity of the student to retain information. Despite its importance the memory has been sadly neglected by educators, although it is essential to learning. Little or no corrective measures have been taken by our educational institutions to correct this deficiency. It is our purpose to fulfill this need.

The brain is like a library where knowledge is stored.

Our ability to retain this knowledge depends upon how well it has become intrenched in our minds. With the aid of the sleep-o-matic units you can remember foreign vocabularies, spelling, historical dates, geographical data, mathematical formulas, chemical formulas, and statistics of all kinds.

YOUR MEMORY CAN BE IMPROVED. A GOOD MEMORY IS NOT A GIFT. IT IS AN ATTAINMENT WHICH IS PROCURED THROUGH TRAINING BASED UPON CORRECT PRINCIPLES. AS YOU EXERCISE AND TRAIN YOUR MEMORY YOU WILL FIND ITS POWER TO RETAIN INFORMATION GREATLY INCREASE.

You Can Be A Better Speaker

Nervousness in public speaking is usually due to the fear of being unable to say just what one wants to say at the right time. One of the essential factors that contributes favorably to the confidence of the speaker is his ability to remember the thoughts he intends to express. Many men and women, with a natural ability for public speaking, are hindered psychologically when talking in public because of the fear of forgetting that which is important to express. This handicap may be readily overcome by improving one's memory. A successful talk requires a good memory. This in turn brings with it added self-confidence and a sense of security. Besides enabling one to talk without notes, the sleep-o-matic units will prove a valuable stimulant to the mind.

MEMORY DEVELOPMENT WHILE YOU SLEEP

You Can Improve Your Memory

Any one can quickly attain an accurate memory. It does not require a special adaptability. The memory is a functioning mechanism and therefore must be exercised and trained if it is to work in a satisfactory manner. Your memory is a remarkable faculty. You have the proper mental equipment; you need only to know how to use it to obtain real improvement.

Psychologists maintain that there is no such thing as a "poor memory" unless the memory faculty is impeded by some organic defect. A so-called weak or poor memory is actually one that is untrained. Your memory, like a muscle in the human body, can be developed and strengthened. This attainment is now within your grasp.

It has been empirically established that the memory and the learning processes are sharpened under the influence of hypnosis. Actually when sleep suggestion is used, normal sleep is changed into hypnotic sleep so that the same results are attained.

The sleep-o-matic units are the instruments through which we convert normal sleep into hypnotic sleep so that through sleep suggestion, we can improve the memory of the sleeper. It is interesting to note that many schools are using this technique in the teaching of languages and other studies. I know many who have successfully used this medium. They are all unanimous in their praise and enthusiasm for this new and exciting method. The following article appeared in the October 24, 1949 issue of the Los Angeles Express:

MENTAL-POWER THROUGH SLEEP-SUGGESTION

EDUCATION THROUGH SUBCONSCIOUS TOLD CLUB

It was proved during the emergencies of war days that students can be far more swiftly educated through their subconscious than through their conscious minds and American boys were given a fluent command of Chinese in three months by such schooling.

That unusual slant on education was brought to Breakfast Bridge Club at its opening meeting of the season by Dr. Kenneth Walker, who served his country during the war by assisting in training American service men.

Dr. Walker declared that the subconscious mind represents nine-tenths of human mentality and the conscious mind only one-tenth.

"Yet education continues to place the main burden on that one-tenth," he said.

Experiments of French psychologists and scientists with conditioning the reflexes of dogs led to the experiments of educators in training the subconscious minds of service men, he said.

Quick Education

"It was necessary to educate many men quickly in foreign languages," he said. "I was trying to teach Chinese which is difficult. By a series of accidents we tried this French school of psychology.

"As a result, phonograph records of the Chinese language were placed under the pillows of students at night. About an hour or two after they went to sleep the records were turned on and played intermittently until approximately one hour before waking.

"After several nights of this, the same lesson was given to the conscious mind. In three months ordinary American boys were fluently speaking Chinese.

"Curiously, they spoke with exactly the same accent that they heard on the record, not with an American accent."

Sleep suggestion for the training of the memory, or for any other constructive purpose, does not require any effort! All that is necessary is that the clock on the unit be set for whatever time the sleeper wants the unit to transmit the memory exercise to him. The rewards for the development of one's mental powers are great while the cost is very nominal. If you have, for instance, a phonograph or tape recorder, all you need in addition is the pre-selector clock. It is a small investment indeed for such great returns in improved memory, strength, and buoyancy of spirit. The sleep-o-matic units have proven a tremendous boon to those who have been slow in grasping their lessons. I am personally acquainted with many actors and actresses who are using the sleep-o-matic units successfully in memorizing their scripts. The following article about Ramon Vinay, the opera singer, is an excellent example of this type of learning.

The following article appeared in the October 16, 1950 issue of TIME.

NEW HELDENTENOR

Burly Tenor Ramon (Otello) Vinay was in a sweat. A Chilean trained for Italian and French opera, he had worked hard for over a year to huff himself into a German-style **Heldentenor**, and he was all set to sing his first Tristan, with Kirsten Flagstad as Isolde. San Franciscans (and Metropolitan Opera General Manager Rudolf Bing, who sorely needs a successor to Lauritz Melchior) were all set to hear him. But a fortnight ago, with debut day almost at hand, Tenor Vinay was bogged down in Chile. A stubborn Santiago de Chile impresario refused to let him leave the country until he fulfilled a delayed engagement. Last week, finally freed by persuasion and compromise, Vinay flew to San Francisco, took his big step; was cheered by audience and critics.

He had rushed in two days late, hurried through two piano rehearsals and one with orchestra. He was not worried about his own role of Tristan—although he had found Wagnerian themes "strange for the Latin ear." HE HAD HELPED HIMSELF TO MEMORIZE HIS ROLE BY SLEEPING WITH THE SPEAKER OF A CEREBROGRAPH (AUTOMATIC RECORD PLAYER) UNDER HIS PILLOW TO EMBED THE MUSIC IN HIS SUBCONSCIOUS. But, not knowing German itself, he expected to have a dreadful time following the other singers and catching his cues. Flagstad ("She was always there prompting me or giving me a signal with her eyes") took care of that.

On the big night, the audience in San Francisco's opera house found huge (6 ft. 2 in., 220 lbs.) and handsome Tenor Vinay visually, if not vocally, a heroic match for Soprano Kirsten Flagstad. Wrote San Francisco **Chronicle** Critic Alfred Frankenstein: "To be sure, (Vinay) did not bring the music all the suppleness and vocal ease one hoped for, but he brought it something else that was almost equally important—a tenderness, lyricism and fragility of expression that, were altogether unprecedented. For once, Tristan's ravings in the third act seemed only five times too long instead of ten or twenty or a hundred." Vinay's phrasing particularly when set off against Flagstad's magnificent subtlety, seemed more memorized than inspired. But that defect might well disappear with time.

"Courtesy of TIME, Copyright Time Inc., 1950"

Children learn language before they are actually familiar with the spoken word. The repeated stimuli entering the nervous system through the sensory receptor of the ear transmit a message to the cerebral cortex. These repeated stimuli establish memory patterns which they then consciously recall. The total integration of these engrams constitute the memory. When the attempt is made to learn consciously, the subconscious mind being already familiar with its content, since the associations have already been formed, shows the way to easy learning in an already established pattern.

These memory patterns remain engraved in the subconscious even though they may have been consciously forgotten. For example, you perhaps may not have been able to recall an acquaintance that you had known at the age of four or five, until a picture of him is shown to you. His identity is then recalled immediately. This is the type of the stimulus-response pattern to which we referred in the previous statement. This logically leads us to the conclusion that the material transferred to the subconscious during the period of sleep serves as a basis for future learning and better memory.

MEMORY DEVELOPMENT WHILE YOU SLEEP

By transmitting knowledge to the subconscious mind through this process of mechanized sleep-suggestion many arduous years can be cut from the educational process. The greatest advantage of sleep-learning is that it eliminates such constantly irritating difficulties as the conscious inability to concentrate while learning. A third of our lives is spent in sleeping. Why should we not profitably employ this valuable time for therapy or study? Such subjects as mathematics, music, and languages can be learned with ease during the hours of sleep and in such a wonderfully easy manner too, through the use of these record suggestions.

The following experiment in sleep-learning was conducted at the University of North Carolina under the direction of Professor Charles R. Elliott. Forty students, all with perfect hearing, were picked for this test case. The group was divided into two sections of twenty students. Each group slept in Professor Elliott's psychological laboratory for three hours. Electroencephalographs were used to test the condition and depth of each student's slumber. One section slept undisturbed, while the other twenty were exposed to a recording containing a list of words which was piped to each individually through the medium of pillow speakers.

When all the students were awakened, they were asked to memorize this list. Those who had heard it previously learned it with incredible rapidity. The others labored falteringly to attain the same end. Professor Elliott concluded therefore that the process of sleep-teaching was similar to that of reteaching material that had once been known and temporarily forgotten.

Information such as multiplication tables, chemical formulas, the Morse code, logarithms, vocabularies, languages, and other subjects can be easily taught through sleep-education. In teaching the Morse code, the Army and Navy have used sleep-education with the most phenominal results. The men literally slept their way to successful achievement in this highly technical field! What a wonderful aid this medium is for those who have poor memories too. Learning is not only made easy but permanent because of the receptive condition under which this learning takes place.

Our recording on "memory development" contains suggestions that will aid you in awakening the memory centers in your mind so that you will be able to retain impressions easier and more quickly than you ever have been able to do before.

The foregoing demonstrations have unquestionably established sleep learning as a marvelously efficient means of education. Those who wish to increase their mental power in the fields of education and memory are strongly urged to avail themselves of the splendid opportunity by obtaining one of the sleep-o-matic units. It is at once the best teacher and economist of labor and time that we know. Let the nostalgia of the old song, "It's Easy to Remember But So Hard to Forget," become a living reality to those who have developed their memory resources through the use of our sleep-o-matic units.

CHAPTER VIII

The Secret of Achieving Success and Happiness

"The Fault, Dear Brutus, Is Not in Our Stars but in Ourselves." Shakespeare

BENJAMIN DISRAELI, the Earl of Beaconsfield, the architect of the British Empire, once said, "The secret of success is constancy of purpose." He could just as well have said, "The secret of success is constancy of purpose and positive thinking," for it is positive thinking, in the last analysis, added to constancy of purpose, that crumbles the walls of any resistance that lies in the path of the determined seeker of an idea or purpose.

Positive thought is the key to achievement. Thoughts, like the proverbial drops of water that wore away the stone, can cut through any problem that it chooses to conquer. It is the brain, after all, that is in the center of control of our whole organism. As the mind goes, so goes the body. This is an axiom we have heard for years, but do we really understand its significance? If we did, we would be a much more healthy nation! If we really appreciated the fact the brain is in control of our whole organism through an intricate system of cellular structure and connections, we would take care to use it in a manner more positive and constructive to our health and purpose!

Such emotions as anger, depression, violence, and fear cause the generation of poisonous compounds in the organism, while pleasant emotions cause the cells to generate energy and so create a correspondent pervasive sense of well-being in the organism. Which do you prefer, a disturbed mind with its *damaging effects* to the organism, or a relaxed happy mind with a healthy body and outlook? Basically the choice is yours. Abuse your mind with negative attitudes and everything looks dark and hopeless; think happily and constructively and all goes well because the proper, constructive forces have been generated in the mind.

Now that we have suggested the prime importance of our minds in thinking and feeling we can proceed to the matter at hand, namely, the secret of achieving success and happiness. Very closely allied to our need for social recognition is the need for the experiencing the feeling of success. Many of us have never realized that this feeling is just as important to us as the need for air, food, and sleep. It is! All of us want to succeed in something. The satisfaction that comes from an achievement is an exhilarating one indeed, not only because it brings self-satisfaction, but because it is usually accompanied by social approval. Success is a great aid in personality growth because it builds self-assurance and social integration, which are the basic pre-requisites of maturation. Once we realize why we think and act in

THE SECRET OF ACHIEVING SUCCESS AND HAPPINESS

certain ways, we are better able to understand ourselves and others and are therefore better equipped to get along with the other members of our complex society. On the other hand, if we develop feelings of inferiority and rejection not only are our social relationships hampered but our personalities become impaired and we are forced to withdraw from the company of our fellow men —defeated and alone.

Personal success itself, of course, has no true value unless it is accompanied by feelings of happiness, and that feeling cannot exist unless we remember at all times that we are living in a world of people who also have their own goals and aspirations. It therefore becomes extremely clear that we must develop a cooperative viewpoint that constantly takes into consideraion other people's needs, ideas, and rights so that we can all live together in a peaceful world.

We are all alike. We all have the basic drives to produce, to survive, to be recognized as individuals, and to be identified with social groups. If our needs are all so similar why do we become so different? The answer lies in the areas of character, without which there can be no sound personality; purpose, without which life has no direction or goal, and action, without which nothing can be accomplished. It is in these three qualities that happiness and success are to be found. Good habits and personal integrity of course lie at the basis of these factors and "make the wheels go round", to use an old expression.

We are thoroughly aware that happiness depends

partly upon the person and partly upon the environment. We are also cognizant of the fact that unhappiness is created through the disintegration of the individual in the sense that there is an absence of integration between the conscious and the subconscious, and ultimately therefore between himself and society. Our first interest, however, is the lack of unity that exists in the individual as an entity, and it is therefore in this area that we will henceforth discuss happiness and success.

Our purpose in this chapter is to show the importance of positive thinking. We have already indicated in the earlier pages of this chapter how the mind controls the destiny of the whole being and we have illustrated the importance of correct attitudes as a major factor in the preservation of our health and in the pursuit of constructive living. We have also indicated that the disintegration of the personality resulted from the blocking off of the subconscious mind from the conscious thus causing the unitary fragmentation of the personality. We have already suggested in a previous chapter how sleep suggestion could overcome this conscious-subconscious severance through the use of the sleep-o-matic units so that positive and constructive attitudes could be transmitted to the sleeper, thus aiding him to become a healthier and more integrated individual. We will now proceed to further discuss the attitudes and methods essential to happiness and success.

Systematic efforts usually are rewarded by success and happiness. History is full of countless stories of

THE SECRET OF ACHIEVING SUCCESS AND HAPPINESS

how poor boys became millionaires. These were the ones who had the visions of the future. At times they were laughed at and much fun was poked at them for their foolish ideas. They experienced heartaches, disappointments, and despair, but in spite of all those obstacles they forged ahead and won the respect and admiration of the entire world. Such men as Edison, the Wright brothers, Woolworth, Carnegie, Ford, and Schwab are only a few of these greats who illustrate my point.

Do not limit your goal or set up personal barriers! Say that things can be done and do them! If you have a goal in life, do not temporize! Try to achieve it in a methodical manner, and you will succeed! I sincerely believe that anything reasonable can be achieved if an individual desires it sufficiently and is willing to work for it. You may have attained your success already because you had set a goal for yourself and have achieved it, or your job may be merely a stepping stone to a future position. In that case familiarize yourself with the requirements of that job and prepare to achieve it. Do not say, "The other fellow always gets the breaks." The probabilities are that he improved himself sufficiently to become worthy of that position. Have you ever noticed that the fellow who constantly complains about the boss is usually the one that is the least ambitious and industrious? He is usually to be found deeply imbedded in the same rut in spite of the passage of the years. Do not dwell on the negative side of things! The difference between achieving success, or being a failure lies in the nature of your thinking. If conditions are not desirable, do something about them! Get a new job or see how you can become more proficient in your present one! What gets people to the top of the financial ladder? Is it knowledge essentially, or is it that they have a driving ambition to succeed? It is certainly an admixture of both! Those people who are on the top in your field, did they get there through thinking negatively? Of course not! Did they not succeed because they constantly thought and planned better ways of improving themselves? I will grant you that you may be tied to your particular job because others are dependent upon you. You may under those conditions feel yourself a victim of circumstances. That sort of thinking leads to inevitable defeat. Just try a little experiment with me. Sit down in a quiet place and go over in your mind what you have read about the dynamic force of positive suggestion. Try it out for only one week on your job, and you will be amazed at the results! Your life and your work will take on a new brightness and interest.

In speaking before various sales organizations I have challenged salesmen to set higher quotas for themselves and to think constructively at all times. I can tell you that the results have been astounding! How it works! They sell much more because their energies and purposes have become more constructively directed. Ask any salesman you know what is his secret of success. You will find the answer has something to do with the "will to win." We have already told you that these suggestions can be implanted in your subconscious while

THE SECRET OF ACHIEVING SUCCESS AND HAPPINESS

you sleep thus eliminating doubt and negative thinking.

Success in life is not necessarily gained only by hard work. You must know where you are going, you must have a planned blue print of your future! Constructive ends are not going to be achieved until they are worked for! Take inventory of your personal assets and capabilities! Start utilizing your subconscious as well as your conscious mind! Stop doubting yourself! You are as good as the next fellow and perhaps more capable! Start implanting these positive suggestions in your subconscious through the utilization of your conscious mind!

Never say die! It's a wonderful philosophy to live by! Be an optimist! Learn to maintain an air of bouyant self-confidence! Feelings of fear create the very conditions that you want to avoid! If all thoughts of fear and negation were cast aside we would all be happier people!

The constructive cultivation of the mind has for many years been sadly neglected. We have many exercises to develop the body and our muscles, but we are sadly lacking in exercises to cultivate and strengthen the mind. It is indeed a sad commentary on the present condition of man. The improvement of the mind assures a more efficient human mechanism. Think of the bright side of things! Think of what you want to achieve! Think of pleasant things and notice the tonic effect on your entire organism. Don't be dependent upon others! Take the initiative yourself! Know that you have a God given mind, and that it is an important part of the spiritual universe and that it contains infinite powers for good! If you fully realize this, you will be free from despair and you will more likely be able to accomplish your goals!

Our thoughts like rubies can be jewels of worth. Our thoughts like diamonds can be sparkling and bright. It is up to us! Have you read the story of Ponce de Leon and his search for the fountain of youth? He searched everywhere and never found it, and why not? Because he searched in the wrong places, for it was to be found only within himself! There lies our strength and our salvation! "You are what you think you are." In that statement lies the wisdom of the ages. When progress is no longer sought, there is no longer an interest in life. Those who lose interest in education and think only in negative terms are like unlit lamps that never burn!

We have all read that matter is composed of molecules, atoms and the smallest known particle, the electron. An atom is said to be so small that a very fine grain of sand contains millions of them. The molecule is made of atoms, which supposedly contain little particles of matter that revolve around one another in a continuous circuit at a speed as fast as light. It is similar to the rotation of the earth and other planets around the sun in an endless circuit. An atom in turn is made up of the electrons which are also in constant motion. You have heard it said, no doubt, that if we could

THE SECRET OF ACHIEVING SUCCESS AND HAPPINESS

harness the energy of the atoms that are in a teaspoon of water, we would have enough power to drive an ocean liner around the world. We can do equally wonderful things once we learn to tap the power of the subconscious mind.

Can you visualize your subconscious mind as containing a powerful dynamo? A dynamo more powerful than Niagara Falls! Can you visualize this dynamic force awakening the sources of power that is within us which would make it possible to achieve success, wealth, and happiness? Once you tap the vast currents of nature's force, that is the subconscious mind, it will supply the irresistible impetus for your goals.

I realize that you may well be skeptical and doubt this monolithic power, but there is infinite psychic power within us that can be used for the good of ourselves and all mankind and that power lies in the connection between our conscious and subconscious mind which can be generated through the dynamism of suggestion.

If you were offered the wonderful gifts of bouyant health, wealth, happiness, and a full and abundant life, you would doubtlessly not hesitate to accept them. The sleep-o-matic units can bring you great gifts by awakening the dormant brain cells, and opening the bounty of the subconscious mind so that your life may become enriched with the enlarged vistas and glorious horizons that are newly opened to eyes that were more or less blinded before!

No one can teach you success. I can teach you how

to become successful, but you can only achieve success when you have found yourself! Until you have developed your latent powers and talents, you will flounder in the mire of confused mediocrity.

Psychology teaches us the art of creative thinking. Very few people however ever do anything about it! It is possible to shake off the old habits and shackles of the past and to create for ourselves an entirely new life, based upon sound proven psychological principles. These principles are embodied in the use of our sleep-o-matic units.

To live the abundant, healthy, and happy life, it is necessary to understand the workings of the laws of psychology. Life is not a haphazard affair; it operates according to a plan. If you want to acquire leadership, you must prepare for it!

Visualize what you want in your mind's eye. This mental picture of your life's plan will work wonders for you! Most people idly think about wanting to be this or that and that is the end of it. Make a mental image of your desires. Picture yourself as having become possessed by them and you will prepare yourself for that achievement. Now I'm not saying that you should be a dreamer and that's all. By all means no! We must also face reality; we must stand the test of everyday living. All great men were dreamers. Goals must be visualized before they can be achieved. All things begin with a mental plan or image. What you do with it is up to yourself. Your thoughts can be dissipated or they

THE SECRET OF ACHIEVING SUCCESS AND HAPPINESS

can be made to achieve the ends you desire. By sleep suggestion you can stimulate the creative powers that lie dormant within your subconscious mind. Sleep suggestion will enable you to generate your thoughts into a pattern of dynamic power which can be used for purposes of constructive and triumphant living.

I once heard a man say he needed a change of scenery because he wasn't getting anywhere in life and yet he was living in the capital of world trade, New York City. I suggested a change of thinking instead. He accepted my advice and today owns much valuable real estate in the city he once thought he didn't like.

Dr. William James, Harvard University's long celebrated psychologist and philosopher, said "There is no more miserable human being than one in whom nothing is habitual but indecision." Once you have made up your mind to achieve a specific goal, keep at it. You will achieve it if you persevere until your goal is reached. If in the pursuit of your goal you find your plan hasn't materialized, try another. The fault may be in your procedure or in the objective you have chosen, or have in view. It is useless and unintelligent to try to achieve the impossible. We make no such suggestions. Goals are important, but make them achievable goals or pain and frustration will be the inevitable result. In a symbolic sense, hitch your wagon to a star. Yes, but make it a star that is not outside the reaches of reasonable achievement so that its realization can be yours.

CHAPTER IX

The Sleep-o-matic Units, the Instruments for Releasing Subconscious Power

"Go Forth to Meet the Shadowy Future Without Fear and with a Manly Heart." Longfellow

WE HAVE come a long way. Our discussion up to this point has covered the area of the subconscious mind in action, the power of suggestion, the use of sleep recorded suggestion for mental-therapy, the development of memory through the same process, and the secret of achieving success and happiness. We have discussed many things. I hope that you have found the comments a source of interest and inspiration. It is now time to get to the practical aspects of the method of sleep suggestion.

The employment of suggestion in learning, mental-therapy, and the improvement of memory has been in existence for a long time. The circumstances under which this procedure was utilized were, however, not always propitious. There were times when elements of tension and interference destroyed the rapport between the two principals, the therapist or teacher, and the patient or student. These unhappy conditions prevailed for a long period of time until the invention of the phonograph and the tape recorder. These remarkable

THE SLEEP-O-MATIC UNITS, THE INSTRUMENTS, FOR RELEASING SUBCONSCIOUS POWER

instruments opened up new possibilities in the field of suggestion. It became possible through the medium of the phonograph recordings and tape recordings to transmit messages in the privacy of one's room under the most favorable circumstances and at any time. This opened the way for sleep suggestion and the splendid opportunities it has made possible in the areas of therapy, learning, and memory training.

The phonograph and tape recorder were great achievements in themselves, but they could not possibly have been of use to us in our field unless the time clock could be used in conjunction with them. It is the special clock on our sleep-o-matic unit. We call it the pre-selector time clock, because it automatically turns the units on or off, thus making sleep transmission of suggestions possible. If sleep suggestion is desired during the night, the best time to set the pre-selector clock is for the first two hours after going to bed, or the last two hours before getting up for these are the hours of deepest sleep. Set the clock for as long or short a period during the night you wish the sleep-o-matic unit to play, and go to sleep as you would normally do, letting the miracle of sleep suggestion bathe and strengthen you with its potent power as you slumber oblivious to everything else in the external world.

The pillow speaker is also a vital adjunct of the two sleep-o-matic units. Its value lies in the fact that it avoids disturbing any one else who might be sleeping in the same room in which the unit is being used. The speaker is placed under the pillow of the sleeper so that no one else gets the effects of the transmission.

For the purpose of clarity and in order to illustrate the usage of our two units, the sleep-o-matic phonograph recorder and the sleep-o-matic tape recorder, let us return for a moment to the subconscious mind for it is through the aforementioned units that the subconscious is freed for positive action. Remember it is not the function of the subconscious mind to reason, but to accept stimuli from the brain and store these stimuli for future use. It, in fact, stores all the repressed ideas and emotions that have ever occurred that we rejected consciously and which we can now release through suggestive therapy and more importantly for us, it is the seat of our illimitable psychic power which is the very life force of our being. It is this life force that our sleep-o-matic units contact during the period of sleep.

During the hours of sleep, as I have explained, the mind is in a passive state and does not serve as an obstacle on the path to the subconscious. The subconscious springs into a highly sensitized and active state as the rest of the organism slips into the unconsciousness of the sleep state. In short, the subconscious becomes accessible to suggestions and influences that are denied to it during the hours when the conscious mind interferes with its effective functioning, so that in that state the psychic phenomena of ideas, emotions,

THE SLEEP-O-MATIC UNITS, THE INSTRUMENTS, FOR RELEASING SUBCONSCIOUS POWER

and the imagination continue to flow with uninhibited ease. The sleep period then is the desirable time for sleep-o-matic use, and that is when we employ it for greatest success.

The weary one goes to bed, he has set his sleep-o-matic so that he will receive contact from it during his sleeping hours. The day has been a hard one; the problems have been many; the boss had been irascible; life doesn't seem worth living. He rests his head on the pillow, and slides into the warm, sweet forgetfulness of sleep. Time goes by, and suddenly at the set moment the recording starts and positive, wonderful suggestions are piped through the pillow speaker into the private ears of the sleeper without in the least disturbing his slumber. The positive, soothing suggestions continue until the unit is automatically turned off by the pre-selector time clock, which has been regulated according to the needs or desires of the sleeper. In the morning, the sleeper awakes, jumps out of bed, and looks around. Somehow the world looks brighter, the problems and sense of depression seem to have vanished! It isn't the usual refreshed feeling that results from a good night's rest, but something new! A new verve, a new force, and purpose have been born! New ideas, new plans come bubbling to the surface of the mind! Thoughts like a new job, new ambition, and new goals sing and vibrate in the regenerated mind, and all because the sleep-o-matic unit has been sending a message of constructive inspirations and suggestions to the beleaguered dream-

MENTAL-POWER THROUGH SLEEP-SUGGESTION

er's subconscious and bidding him to grasp this thing called "Life" with courage and purpose. This contact and renewal of positive suggestions repeated night after night have incalculable results for the person hitherto confused. His attitude towards himself and life have undergone a constructive revolutionary change! He is a new man, and is so because his conscious and subconscious minds are in full harmony with one another, and as I have already suggested, that is the mark of the integrated and happy man.

The repetition of positive messages to the subconscious makes that instrument a source of power, happiness, and success. I can not emphasize this basic truth too often! This is not mere theory! Thoughts and feelings are intangible and subtle. Have you heard of anyone, no matter how gifted, who could put his finger on a thought? Of course not! Nobody has ever seen the flash of a thought, and yet the mind flashes, crackles, and generates thoughts like a dynamo creates electricity. It is this latent force that is awakened through suggestion and the controlled power of our sleep-o-matic units.

Please note that when we speak of the sleep-o-matic units, we are actually referring to two types of that unit. One, the phonograph sleep-o-matic unit, which has a pre-selector time clock and a pillow-speaker attachment, which is used under the pillow of the sleeper and two, the tape recorder sleep-o-matic unit which also utilizes a pre-selector time clock and pillow speaker attachment and which are used the same way as in the former unit.

THE SLEEP-O-MATIC UNITS, THE INSTRUMENTS, FOR RELEASING SUBCONSCIOUS POWER

We have introduced two units because there are those who may already have either a phonograph or a tape recorder and so would only require a pre-selector time clock and pillow speaker to make up a complete sleep-o-matic unit.

The phonograph sleep-o-matic unit has use also as a regular phonograph player and is able to play records of any type and speed. It is a first class musical instrument as well. The clock can also be used for the usual purposes such as telling time, turning on various appliances, and when connected with the radio can serve the same purpose as an alarm clock in the morning. You would then awaken to your favorite morning radio program. The tape recorder can also be used for purposes other than that of sleep suggestion. It can be utilized as a source of sound for home movies, for dictation, as a means of improving speech, for recording favorite records or shows that are played on the radio or on television. It can also be used for an evening's entertainment.

The two instruments are versatile indeed, and as you readily see can be used in many ways, but their greatest benefit lies in the area of sleep suggestion and the strengthening of the personality, for that, after all, has been the main objective of this book.

MENTAL-POWER THROUGH SLEEP-SUGGESTION

Our various sleep-o-matic recordings contain suggestions which will aid you in achieving your goals and aspirations. These records and tapes, although utilized most effectively during the hours of sleep as I have already indicated in this book, can also be used beneficially during the waking hours when conditions of complete relaxation prevail. Upon request, I shall be pleased to send you a catalogue describing the various sleep-o-matic records, sleep-o-matic units, and accessories. Write to: Melvin Powers, 12015 Sherman Road, No. Hollywood, California 91605.

Don't face tomorrow with yesterday's deficiencies! The future is largely in your own hands! It is yours to do with what you will! We end with the words of the illustrious poet, Philip James Bailey:

> Let each man think himself an act of God,
> His mind a thought, his life a breath of God;
> And let each try, by great thoughts and good deeds,
> To show the most of heaven, he hath in him.

MELVIN POWERS SELF-IMPROVEMENT LIBRARY

BUSINESS, STUDY & REFERENCE

____ CONVERSATION MADE EASY *Elliot Russell*	4.00
____ EXAM SECRET *Dennis B. Jackson*	3.00
____ FIX-IT BOOK *Arthur Symons*	2.00
____ HOW TO DEVELOP A BETTER SPEAKING VOICE *M. Hellier*	4.00
____ HOW TO SELF-PUBLISH YOUR BOOK & MAKE IT A BEST SELLER *Melvin Powers*	10.00
____ INCREASE YOUR LEARNING POWER *Geoffrey A. Dudley*	3.00
____ PRACTICAL GUIDE TO BETTER CONCENTRATION *Melvin Powers*	3.00
____ PRACTICAL GUIDE TO PUBLIC SPEAKING *Maurice Forley*	5.00
____ 7 DAYS TO FASTER READING *William S. Schaill*	3.00
____ SONGWRITERS' RHYMING DICTIONARY *Jane Shaw Whitfield*	6.00
____ SPELLING MADE EASY *Lester D. Basch & Dr. Milton Finkelstein*	3.00
____ STUDENT'S GUIDE TO BETTER GRADES *J. A. Rickard*	3.00
____ TEST YOURSELF—Find Your Hidden Talent *Jack Shafer*	3.00
____ YOUR WILL & WHAT TO DO ABOUT IT *Attorney Samuel G. Kling*	4.00

HOBBIES

____ BEACHCOMBING FOR BEGINNERS *Norman Hickin*	2.00
____ BLACKSTONE'S MODERN CARD TRICKS *Harry Blackstone*	3.00
____ BLACKSTONE'S SECRETS OF MAGIC *Harry Blackstone*	3.00
____ COIN COLLECTING FOR BEGINNERS *Burton Hobson & Fred Reinfeld*	3.00
____ ENTERTAINING WITH ESP *Tony 'Doc' Shiels*	2.00
____ 400 FASCINATING MAGIC TRICKS YOU CAN DO *Howard Thurston*	4.00
____ HOW I TURN JUNK INTO FUN AND PROFIT *Sari*	3.00
____ HOW TO WRITE A HIT SONG & SELL IT *Tommy Boyce*	7.00
____ JUGGLING MADE EASY *Rudolf Dittrich*	3.00
____ MAGIC FOR ALL AGES *Walter Gibson*	4.00
____ MAGIC MADE EASY *Byron Wels*	2.00
____ STAMP COLLECTING FOR BEGINNERS *Burton Hobson*	3.00

HYPNOTISM

____ ADVANCED TECHNIQUES OF HYPNOSIS *Melvin Powers*	3.00
____ BRAINWASHING AND THE CULTS *Paul A. Verdier, Ph.D.*	3.00
____ CHILDBIRTH WITH HYPNOSIS *William S. Kroger, M.D.*	5.00
____ HOW TO SOLVE Your Sex Problems with Self-Hypnosis *Frank S. Caprio, M.D.*	5.00
____ HOW TO STOP SMOKING THRU SELF-HYPNOSIS *Leslie M. LeCron*	3.00
____ HOW TO USE AUTO-SUGGESTION EFFECTIVELY *John Duckworth*	3.00
____ HOW YOU CAN BOWL BETTER USING SELF-HYPNOSIS *Jack Heise*	4.00
____ HOW YOU CAN PLAY BETTER GOLF USING SELF-HYPNOSIS *Jack Heise*	3.00
____ HYPNOSIS AND SELF-HYPNOSIS *Bernard Hollander, M.D.*	5.00
____ HYPNOTISM *(Originally published in 1893)* *Carl Sextus*	5.00
____ HYPNOTISM & PSYCHIC PHENOMENA *Simeon Edmunds*	4.00
____ HYPNOTISM MADE EASY *Dr. Ralph Winn*	5.00
____ HYPNOTISM MADE PRACTICAL *Louis Orton*	5.00
____ HYPNOTISM REVEALED *Melvin Powers*	2.00
____ HYPNOTISM TODAY *Leslie LeCron and Jean Bordeaux, Ph.D.*	5.00
____ MODERN HYPNOSIS *Lesley Kuhn & Salvatore Russo, Ph.D.*	5.00
____ NEW CONCEPTS OF HYPNOSIS *Bernard C. Gindes, M.D.*	5.00
____ NEW SELF-HYPNOSIS *Paul Adams*	5.00
____ POST-HYPNOTIC INSTRUCTIONS—Suggestions for Therapy *Arnold Furst*	5.00
____ PRACTICAL GUIDE TO SELF-HYPNOSIS *Melvin Powers*	3.00
____ PRACTICAL HYPNOTISM *Philip Magonet, M.D.*	3.00
____ SECRETS OF HYPNOTISM *S. J. Van Pelt, M.D.*	5.00
____ SELF-HYPNOSIS A Conditioned-Response Technique *Laurence Sparks*	7.00
____ SELF-HYPNOSIS Its Theory, Technique & Application *Melvin Powers*	3.00
____ THERAPY THROUGH HYPNOSIS *edited by Raphael H. Rhodes*	5.00

SELF-HELP & INSPIRATIONAL

____ DAILY POWER FOR JOYFUL LIVING *Dr. Donald Curtis*	5.00
____ DYNAMIC THINKING *Melvin Powers*	2.00

___	GREATEST POWER IN THE UNIVERSE *U. S. Andersen*	5.00
___	GROW RICH WHILE YOU SLEEP *Ben Sweetland*	3.00
___	GROWTH THROUGH REASON *Albert Ellis, Ph.D.*	4.00
___	GUIDE TO PERSONAL HAPPINESS *Albert Ellis, Ph.D. & Irving Becker, Ed. D.*	5.00
___	HELPING YOURSELF WITH APPLIED PSYCHOLOGY *R. Henderson*	2.00
___	HOW TO ATTRACT GOOD LUCK *A. H. Z. Carr*	5.00
___	HOW TO DEVELOP A WINNING PERSONALITY *Martin Panzer*	5.00
___	HOW TO DEVELOP AN EXCEPTIONAL MEMORY *Young & Gibson*	5.00
___	HOW TO LIVE WITH A NEUROTIC *Albert Ellis, Ph. D.*	5.00
___	HOW TO OVERCOME YOUR FEARS *M. P. Leahy, M.D.*	3.00
___	HUMAN PROBLEMS & HOW TO SOLVE THEM *Dr. Donald Curtis*	5.00
___	I CAN *Ben Sweetland*	7.00
___	I WILL *Ben Sweetland*	3.00
___	LEFT-HANDED PEOPLE *Michael Barsley*	5.00
___	MAGIC IN YOUR MIND *U. S. Andersen*	6.00
___	MAGIC OF THINKING BIG *Dr. David J. Schwartz*	3.00
___	MAGIC POWER OF YOUR MIND *Walter M. Germain*	5.00
___	MENTAL POWER THROUGH SLEEP SUGGESTION *Melvin Powers*	3.00
___	NEW GUIDE TO RATIONAL LIVING *Albert Ellis, Ph.D. & R. Harper, Ph.D.*	3.00
___	PROJECT YOU *A Manual of Rational Assertiveness Training Paris & Casey*	6.00
___	PSYCHO-CYBERNETICS *Maxwell Maltz, M.D.*	5.00
___	SCIENCE OF MIND IN DAILY LIVING *Dr. Donald Curtis*	5.00
___	SECRET OF SECRETS *U. S. Andersen*	6.00
___	SECRET POWER OF THE PYRAMIDS *U. S. Andersen*	5.00
___	STUTTERING AND WHAT YOU CAN DO ABOUT IT *W. Johnson, Ph.D.*	2.50
___	SUCCESS-CYBERNETICS *U. S. Andersen*	6.00
___	10 DAYS TO A GREAT NEW LIFE *William E. Edwards*	3.00
___	THINK AND GROW RICH *Napoleon Hill*	5.00
___	THINK YOUR WAY TO SUCCESS *Dr. Lew Losoncy*	5.00
___	THREE MAGIC WORDS *U. S. Andersen*	5.00
___	TREASURY OF COMFORT *edited by Rabbi Sidney Greenberg*	5.00
___	TREASURY OF THE ART OF LIVING *Sidney S. Greenberg*	5.00
___	YOU ARE NOT THE TARGET *Laura Huxley*	5.00
___	YOUR SUBCONSCIOUS POWER *Charles M. Simmons*	5.00
___	YOUR THOUGHTS CAN CHANGE YOUR LIFE *Dr. Donald Curtis*	5.00

SPORTS

___	BICYCLING FOR FUN AND GOOD HEALTH *Kenneth E. Luther*	2.00
___	BILLIARDS—Pocket • Carom • Three Cushion *Clive Cottingham, Jr.*	3.00
___	CAMPING-OUT 101 Ideas & Activities *Bruno Knobel*	2.00
___	COMPLETE GUIDE TO FISHING *Vlad Evanoff*	2.00
___	HOW TO IMPROVE YOUR RACQUETBALL *Lubarsky Kaufman & Scagnetti*	3.00
___	HOW TO WIN AT POCKET BILLIARDS *Edward D. Knuchell*	5.00
___	JOY OF WALKING *Jack Scagnetti*	3.00
___	LEARNING & TEACHING SOCCER SKILLS *Eric Worthington*	3.00
___	MOTORCYCLING FOR BEGINNERS *I. G. Edmonds*	3.00
___	RACQUETBALL FOR WOMEN *Toni Hudson, Jack Scagnetti & Vince Rondone*	3.00
___	RACQUETBALL MADE EASY *Steve Lubarsky, Rod Delson & Jack Scagnetti*	4.00
___	SECRET OF BOWLING STRIKES *Dawson Taylor*	3.00
___	SECRET OF PERFECT PUTTING *Horton Smith & Dawson Taylor*	3.00
___	SOCCER—The Game & How to Play It *Gary Rosenthal*	3.00
___	STARTING SOCCER *Edward F. Dolan, Jr.*	3.00

The books listed above can be obtained from your book dealer or directly from Melvin Powers. When ordering, please remit 50¢ per book postage & handling. Send for our free illustrated catalog of self-improvement books.

Melvin Powers

12015 Sherman Road, No. Hollywood, California 91605